THE 7Cs OF LEADERSHIP MASTERY

Also by Claudine Pereira

"Top 10 Lessons Learned,"
in *The Sisterhood Folios: Live Out Loud.*
Star House Press, 2017

THE 7Cs OF LEADERSHIP MASTERY

Unleash The Leader in You

CLAUDINE PEREIRA

THE PINK COACH
UNIVERSITY

For information regarding permissions and bulk purchases, please contact:
info@thepinkcoach.com

ISBN Paperback 978-1-0690196-3-9
ISBN Hardcover 978-1-0690196-2-2
ISBN Ebook 978-1-0690196-1-5
ISBN Audio 978-1-0690196-4-6

Cover and interior design by Big World Creative

DEDICATION

I dedicate this book to the countless unsung leaders around the world, whose impactful and deliberate contributions often go unnoticed and unrewarded. My hope is that this book will awaken the leadership potential within each of you, serving as a reminder that greatness is within reach, ready to be discovered and embraced. Will you rise to the challenge?

To Monica and Alyson: your early influence ignited my leadership journey. Thank you for planting the seeds of great leadership within me. I will be eternally grateful.

Coach Judi: the cornerstone of my success—I am never leaving you!

TABLE OF CONTENTS

PREFACE

lead·er·ship

noun

The action of leading a group of people or an organization.

The state or position of being a leader.

The capacity to lead; the ability to guide, direct, or influence others.

Upon reflection, I realize that I had inspirational leadership heroes around me right from the beginning. Now here I am in 2024 after ten years of running my own business following a lifetime working in various management roles and benefiting from the daily grind of deliberate leadership. Everyday leadership is needed.

I've been blessed with learning from amazing leaders over the years and in the following pages, I'm going to share my leadership journey with you, But, first, let me introduce you to here are some of my first early inspirational leaders and role models.

Growing up in the UK, I daydreamed about living the American Dream. My life revolved around dancing Mo's Place in Reading, England. I loved this beyond anything at. My favourite shows were Dallas and Dynasty. Joan Collins—who today is 90+ in age—remains the ultimate female leader. I fell in love with her sassy swagger, style, and powerful leadership as a woman. I wanted some of that, I just didn't know what to do to get there.

I pictured living in a nice home, shopping, and having a marvelous high-powered job where I could also dress up and in expensive clothes and shoes, just like my idol. For me, Joan Collins blew out of the water the idea of heroic white male-dominated leaders and inspired me to work harder. What I hadn't appreciated was the goal setting, coordination of knowledge, and the huge amount of commitment I gave to dance was already instilling in me sustainable leadership traits miles apart from the "hero leader model" of the day.

My dream did come true. My leadership journey began at the tender age of 23 when I migrated to Canada. Armed with ambition and a hunger for growth, I stepped into the corporate world, ready to navigate the complexities of leading teams and making impactful decisions—in my power dresses and high heels. I had no clue what I was doing or what was ahead of me. I did have a passion for people; and so my journey began.

The early days were a crucible of experiences, a melting pot where I encountered both the brilliance and shadows of leadership. I found myself in the unique position of learning not only from exemplary leaders (massive shout out here to Alyson, who saw something in me and took a risk), but also from those who, perhaps unwittingly, revealed the pitfalls of misguided leadership. I will change names, but you will get the gist of how poor behaviours from certain so-called "leaders" affected me, what was happening to me, and what some of which undoubtedly continues to happen to this day.

My book, The 7Cs of Leadership Mastery, is born from my own experiences. It is a compendium of lessons learned through the trials and triumphs of leadership; a reflection of the growth that I experienced as an employee and now as a successful leader in my business.

As I ascended the corporate ranks, I bore witness to the dance between success and failure, observed the subtle choreography of effective leadership, and both positive and negative impacts that one person can have on an entire team. Through it all, these seven guiding principles emerged. The seven are cornerstones that, when embraced, form the foundations of my own situational leadership style and how I lead others through my transformative coaching programs.

This journey has been a picture woven with encounters, conversations, victories, and defeats. Each colour and image represents a lesson learned, a revelation about the essence of leadership. The 7 Cs—Credibility Communication Compassion Courage Creativity Customer Change—serve as beacons, illuminating the path toward leadership excellence. Leadership is a personal choice. It isn't about authority. It's a way of life, a choice. As women in leadership, we need to lead from behind, not from the front, so we can see what's ahead of us and guide our teams effectively. Likewise, men in leadership can benefit from this approach, ensuring they stay attuned to their team's needs and the challenges ahead.

Navigating The Way Through Calm and Stormy Waters

Imagine you're standing at the helm of a ship, navigating through uncharted waters. As a leader, your role is to steer your team toward success with clarity, confidence, and compassion. Just like a captain relies on the compass to guide their ship, you must rely on your values and vision as your compass to guide your team. Embrace the challenges as opportunities for growth and remember: the journey is just as important as the destination. Lead with courage, communicate with clarity, and empower your team to sail toward greatness. You have the power to chart a course that inspires, motivates, and empowers others to reach new horizons. You are the captain of your ship, and your leadership sets the course for your team's success.

In the pages that follow, I invite you to embark on a journey of discovery. Whether you are a seasoned or aspiring leader, a business owner, or simply curious about the art of leadership, this book aims to be your guide and make you think. It is a testament to my strong belief that leadership is not confined to a title or corner office but is a continual evolution—one that requires reflection, adaptation, and a commitment to mastery. As John Maynard Keynes said:

"The difficulty lies not so much in developing new ideas as escaping old ones."

I hope these pages inspire, challenge, and equip you with the insights needed to lead with purpose and positive impact. As we delve into the 7Cs let us navigate the intricate dance of leadership together and, in doing so, unlock the potential within ourselves and those we have the privilege to lead.

To my point of view, leadership is a way of life. Whether you are a business owner, managing a team, or just a human being living life, you can lead. The best leaders I have ever met have no title. Imagine if we had a world filled with a diverse range of leaders and unsung heroes, what a planet this would be.

It has and will continue to be my mission to create new and upcoming leaders in this world. I hope this book travels far and wide and lands in the hands of those who feel they would never shine. Well, guess what? You can and it's time! Leadership is all about positive influences, full stop.

Let's dive into the 7Cs together and ride the leadership wave!

INTRODUCTION

We often think that leadership is synonymous with management, which involves overseeing day-to-day operations, ensuring tasks are completed efficiently, and meeting organizational goals. However, this view only captures a part of what true leadership entails. Management focuses primarily on maintaining the status quo, whereas leadership encompasses skills that enable individuals to inspire and motivate others.

Management is often concerned with ensuring that processes, systems, and structures run smoothly and efficiently. Managers typically focus on:

Planning and Organizing	Developing detailed plans to achieve organizational goals and ensuring that resources are allocated appropriately.
Controlling and Monitoring	Setting performance standards, monitoring progress, and implementing corrective actions to stay on track.
Consistency and Stability	Maintaining established policies and procedures to ensure predictability and order within the organization.

On the other hand, leadership is about envisioning the future and inspiring people to move towards it. Leaders are characterized by their ability to:

Inspire and Motivate	Creating a compelling vision that excites and energizes others. Leaders connect with their team on an emotional level, fostering a sense of purpose and commitment.
Drive Change	Challenging the status quo and encouraging innovation. Leaders are willing to take risks and push boundaries to achieve greater success.
Empower and Develop	Investing in the growth and development of their team members. Leaders provide support, mentorship, and opportunities for individuals to reach their full potential.

In essence, while management ensures that the current operations are efficient and effective, leadership is about paving the way for future growth and transformation. Both roles are crucial, but it's the combination of strong management and inspiring leadership that drives sustainable success and progress in any organization.

Leadership extends far beyond the duties included in management. Leadership involves inspiring innovation and encouraging individuals to navigate through challenges with creativity. Leaders focus on creating an environment where team members feel empowered to think outside of the box and propose novel solutions to problems. By promoting continuous learning and providing the resources necessary for innovation, leaders can drive their teams and organizations toward transformative growth and success. This kind of leadership exudes credibility, communication, compassion, courage, customer appreciation, change, and creativity in everything they touch!

HOW TO USE THIS BOOK

Whether you are new to leadership, entering the leadership world as a business owner or a corporate manager, this book will give you the tactics to guide you in the leadership journey. It is a refresher for some. It is in an order for a reason, and it is my recommendation that you read it as presented, however if a particular chapter jumps out at you, go to that chapter first and then return to the beginning.

I would encourage that you take some sidenotes in terms of noting what is jumping out at you, what you are already doing, and what you need to work on. Answer the questions honestly and make a plan of action to close that loop.

I'd love for you to share this book and the concepts with others as this is what leaders do.

Now let's dive in!

1c
COMMUNICATION

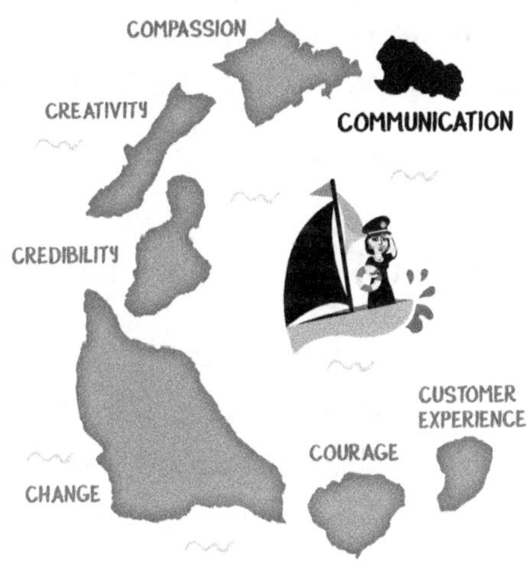

"The single biggest problem in communication
is the illusion that it has taken place."

- George Bernard Shaw

COMMUNICATION CODE

- Share information clearly and quickly in a transparent and honest way
- Adapt your style according to your audience and respect differences
- Ask questions, be interested, and listen

Communication: A Leadership Mindset

Have you ever felt that you have carefully crafted your message, but then become aware that there is still confusion with your audience? Me too! It's a common occurrence. Transformational leadership involves openly sharing your beliefs and knowledge and facilitating a collective transformation with others. Share information clearly and quickly transparently and honestly. Let's explore together the importance of communication as a leader.

THE POWER OF TRANSPARENCY

Transparency builds trust. When leaders communicate openly about their goals, along with the challenges requiring them to set those goals as well as the challenges they expect the team will have to meet them, it garners respect. Leaders who are clear about their expectations fosters a culture of trust and mutual respect within their teams and organizations. Alyson was one of my first mentors and I've mentioned her frequently in these pages. She used to coach me and remind me always to be honest with my team and explain the "why" behind what we are asking them to do, particularly if we expected resistance. Difficult, yes, however, I always found my teams had respect for the direction or decision even if they disagreed. At times, as a leader, you may disagree with a track you have to lead your team through; but if you back up your message, the trust you gain is powerful.

Be honest about both successes and failures. This not only builds credibility, but it also encourages your team to feel community with you as they see that they are working with you through your own learning and improvement, thus feel freer to take the risk of learning new things and improving, too.

One of my big fears going into leadership was being fully transparent—and this was not because I wanted to be deceptive. Rather it was because I was afraid of how telling the full truth of the situation and how it might be received because I desperately wanted to be liked as a leader.

Big mistake. That people-pleasing trait is so common and can lead you to unwise choices if you elect to go down the path of least resistance rather than lead to a path which though bumpy, is more likely to get your team and business to a better, more successful place.

One thing I learned on my journey is that the truth is best sugar-coated by the "why we are doing things this way." I became known for delivering the worst of messages, and to this day I coach and encourage my leadership clients to be fully honest with their teams, even at the risk of not being liked, yet respected for their courage.

FEEDBACK LOOPS

Establish regular feedback loops to ensure that your message is being received and understood as intended. This can involve asking for feedback in meetings, conducting surveys, or having one-on-one conversations. The most successful leaders I coach are all holding regularly scheduled 1:1 meetings with their team members to discuss performance and just plain old life in general. Giving regular and timely feedback removes any confusion over performance and expectations. It is a huge boost to your employees as you have carved out time to hear them out.

Communication + Engagement = a happy employee.

Use feedback to refine your communication strategies. Adapt your approach based on the needs and preferences of your audience.

CONSISTENCY IS KEY

Consistency in messaging is crucial. Reiterate key points across different platforms and formats to ensure that the message sticks. Align your verbal and non-verbal communication. Your body language, tone of voice, and facial expressions should reinforce your words. Remember: Snow White never has a bad day!

EMPATHY IN COMMUNICATION

Practice empathetic communication by putting yourself in your audience's shoes. Understand their perspectives, concerns, and emotions. Respond with empathy, showing that you value their input and are genuinely interested in their well-being. Because empathy is so important in communications, we will be expanding on the topic and featuring both empathy and compassion as the topic of an entire chapter.

STORYTELLING

I love a good story. And I tell them often during my keynotes to paint a picture and a visual of the message I'm trying to convey.

Think about a time someone told you a story about a situation and you have never forgotten it. Use storytelling to make your messages more relatable and memorable. Stories can illustrate your points more vividly than abstract concepts and can help to engage your audience emotionally.

Share personal experiences and success stories to inspire and motivate your teams, or if you are a business owner, share with fellow entrepreneurs in your community.

CLARITY AND BREVITY

Strive for clarity and brevity in your communications. Avoid unnecessary jargon and get to the point quickly. This one is a challenge for me, as I love to go "around the houses" to tell my stories. Therefore, getting to know your audience is critical. Jargon and cliches that might unite your team in one area and get your message across quicker but you have to be very aware that they can do the opposite if you misjudge your audience. Such phrases may cause confusion instead—how many of you understood that British expression ("around the houses") right away, and how many of you were a bit stumped at first and had to take a bit of time to figure out my intended meaning?

Use visual aids, such as charts and graphs, to simplify complex information and make it more digestible.

OPEN-DOOR POLICY

Encourage an open-door policy where team members feel comfortable approaching you with their ideas, questions, and concerns. Over the years and to this day with my clients I hear, "but Coach, I am just too busy for these interruptions." This is where 1:1 time is so critical with your people. Daily weekly, monthly scheduled time will mean less interruptions, not more, whether or not you encourage people to come to you. Create that open door policy platform as the openness fosters a culture of inclusivity and collaboration, enhancing overall communication within the team.

REGULAR UPDATES

Keep your team informed with regular updates about projects, company news, and any changes that may affect them. Show them the big picture and get them involved as much as you can. Employees that feel part of the overall culture and have a role to play in the growth of the organization are more likely to be engaged and stay loyal to you. This goes even for small business, where this culture is more important than ever before. Use multiple channels, such as emails, meetings, and newsletters, to ensure that the information reaches everyone.

KNOW YOUR STYLE

During my corporate days, I often wondered, "Why should they listen to me"? Why indeed. We need to craft our communication with understanding for others and compassion for the message being received.

Because of my British accent and how it is perceived in North America, I was often called upon to deliver the worst messages. This accent seems to be a balm despite the message! It wasn't just the accent, of course, but I did develop a knack for getting the communication across but leaving people intact. I always confronted the fear of failing but took the time to carefully craft my message. Although I was a seasoned leader at that time, it was, and still is today "Day 1 of Leadership" every single day. Every day I wake I pretend this is my first day of leadership. You must keep getting better and hone your craft.

I love this leadership/communication moment courtesy of Royal Caribbean Cruises. I was at their private island Coco Cay in the Bahamas, heading to the food and beverage area. It was 11am, and the team I was coaching was having a huddle, getting fired up and clear on their roles for the day with lots of enthusiasm and gusto. Dressed in pristine pink tops (yes on point with the brand), they broke away and headed to their duties with pride. From the chefs taking pride and photos of their newly made hot food counter to the gentlemen sweeping the floor, they were clear on their roles and took each on with complete pride, completely leading, with no titles and a smile!

My most successful clients are the ones who go the extra mile to communicate daily, in person with their teams (or videoconferencing if this is not possible). They start the day off ensuring their team has been heard, and not via an email, or chat tool.

YOU'VE GOT TO ADAPT

Effective communication requires adaptability. Not everyone communicates in the same way, so it's essential to be flexible in your approach. We are all coming to the table with cultural differences and different communication styles. Isn't that a wonderful thing? Life would be a bore if we were all the same.

My first leadership role was in the wonderful cosmopolitan city of Toronto, Canada which is full of so many different cultures. During a coaching session with a new team member, they were having difficulty keeping eye contact with me, and presented to me as aloof. I tried to continue to reach them and even gave my hand after for a shake, which was swiftly ignored. Bizarre. In my mind I thought I was doing a great job communicating to him, so where was I missing the mark, or was I?

Later that day, he returned to tell me that it was against their religion to make eye contact with women. Meanwhile, I was jumping to all kinds of conclusions instead of seeking first to understand. Huge lesson. Human nature always leads us to make judgments and assumptions. And these days, everyone is coming to the workplace with lots of issues, so be kind and seek first to understand the person in front of you.

Consider tailoring your communication style to suit the needs of your audience, whether it's a one-on-one conversation, a team meeting, or a presentation. By being adaptable, you can ensure that your message is received and understood by everyone. And if in doubt ask. Ask questions, be interested, listen and feedback

OPEN YOUR EARS AND REALLY LISTEN

Ask yourself this question, are we listening, or just biting our tongue to get our thoughts out before the person even finishes? Come on! Fess up—that's you, isn't it? Effective communication is a two-way street. It's not just about conveying your message; it's also about listening to others. And that is hard! To this day as a coach, I am tempted to go into rescue mode with my clients. Active listening involves fully concentrating, understanding, responding, and then remembering what is being said. When you listen actively, you show respect and empathy towards others, which can help build stronger relationships and improve teamwork.

Each time I was given the honor of leading a new team, my first goal was to speak less and listen more. Conducting one-on-ones with each employee to find out their likes, and dislikes and setting the stage for our new relationship was a crucial piece of the leadership puzzle. I always wanted to gain their trust from Day 1. Now, they may not have always liked what I had to say, but they knew they were heard.

So many times, I used to hear from disgruntled employees that no one ever heard them out, no one in management was interested in their ideas. Today, if you are leader or an entrepreneur with a team, this to me is table stakes. Listen, listen, and then listen more—especially to new employees as they are critical to the success of your team. You would be surprised to hear how much they have to offer even though they just began their role. It's common to hear, "I just hired them, why did they quit so quickly?" Recent studies show that including our new employees in the business journey early on will keep them engaged from day 1 and feel that they are a part of the bigger picture.

FEEDBACK AS SOON AS YOU CAN

Feedback is a crucial component of communication. It provides individuals with valuable information about their performance, helping them improve and grow. As a leader, it is essential to provide regular feedback to your team members, both positive and constructive. Recognizing their achievements and efforts can boost morale and motivation, leading to increased productivity and job satisfaction. Studies show that the highest-performing teams are being coached by their leaders. (insert stats here).

And don't forget the genuine, on-the-spot, on-the-fly compliments: "I love what you just told the client. You really connected with them when you said..." Be generous with your compliments and be specific. Stay clear of the generic pats on the back, aka, "good job!" What does that really mean?

Asking clarifying questions are a good way to understand what the other person is trying to convey. "So just to clarify, what I am hearing you say is that you are struggling with meeting your sales and you would like more objection handling training". This gives them a chance to offer additional commentary so there is a clear understanding between both parties.

CASE STUDY

I was once approached by a very confident, bold leader named Alejandro during a training session I was conducting on leadership. He was proud of his coaching abilities, but he confided in me that his team didn't appreciate his coaching style. "Por Quoi?" I asked, intrigued. As we delved deeper, it became clear why his employees were disengaged. Alejandro's idea of coaching was sending terse emails like the one he showed me:

From: Alejandro

To: Employee

Subject: Coaching

Morning! I found an error yesterday on your file number 1234567. You failed to obtain the license number, and I noticed this has been a habit this month. Please make sure you follow the guidelines next time.

This form of feedback was problematic. It was impersonal and easy to misconstrue. In an age where leadership is about connection and empathy, such cold, distant communication was a big no-no.

I decided to meet Alejandro in his office, a sleek, modern space with glass walls and minimalist decor. As the sun set, casting a warm glow over the city skyline visible through his floor-to-ceiling windows, we discussed the importance of delivering feedback in a more personal and constructive manner. "How about face-to-face, on-the-spot feedback?" I suggested. "If you're remote, use the phone or a video call." I also suggested regularly scheduled 1 on 1 coaching sessions, which should be face-to-face and contain a well-balanced diet of positive and corrective feedback.

Alejandro listened, but his response was disheartening. "My team just likes me to tell it the way it is," he insisted, crossing his arms and leaning back in his leather chair. I could sense his resistance, a wall built by ego and a reluctance to change.

Despite my efforts to coach Alejandro on adopting a more empathetic approach, he remained steadfast in his ways. I explained how crucial it was to check his ego at the door and truly engage with his team. However, Alejandro's unwillingness to adapt led to a significant career-limiting move. Eventually, he was moved to a different role, one with less responsibility and a smaller team, as his leadership style was not conducive to a positive work environment.

The lesson here is clear: superb leadership requires humility and the ability to adapt. Feedback should be delivered with empathy and a personal touch. Alejandro's story is a poignant reminder that to be a successful leader, one must be willing to grow and evolve, leaving ego behind.

COACHING MOMENT

There is a distinct difference between feedback and coaching. Employees fear coaching because they think they are yet again going to receive corrective feedback. Feedback is positive or corrective. It is on the spot and in the moment

Coaching is a regularly scheduled meeting for the employee to discuss results and personal development plans. Luckily, during my years of working on my communication skills, I loved people and lived to see my employees perform and be their best. Coaching was the best part of my job, and sometimes I tripped over difficult conversations, but I did my best to be honest and leave the person feeling valued, not destroyed, at the end of the conversation.

If you aren't sure of how to deliver a message or what to say, preparation is key. Don't forget we are all human at the end of the day. How would you like this message to be delivered to you? Think about the why, the delivery, and how you want them to feel once the message is out. Prepare for objections and have a Q&A prepared. It is better to over-prepare than under. Role-playing is an effective tool, awkward but great practice. Quite often, the most awful message that I lost sleep over was well received because I was prepared (and because of the accent lol)!

Communication is an ongoing ever learning part of life, here are my favourite top ten tips around the topic.

TIP #1: **Active** **Listening**	**Explanation:** This involves fully concentrating, understanding, responding, and remembering what is being said. Active listening ensures that you accurately grasp the message and respond appropriately. I love asking clarifying questions, "so if I understand correctly what I'm hearing you say is" **Importance:** It fosters mutual respect and understanding, crucial for effective leadership.
TIP #2: **Clarity and** **Conciseness**	**Explanation:** Communicate your message clearly and directly without unnecessary information. Leave out the fluff and get directly to the point! Once you get to know your clients or team, you can tailor your communication style to their personality (now that's another book)! **Importance:** It helps prevent misunderstandings and ensures that your message is understood quickly and accurately.

TIP #3: **Nonverbal** **Communication**	**Explanation:** This includes body language, facial expressions, gestures, and eye contact. Hugely important to ensure we aren't conveying the wrong signs, especially if you live in an online world. **Importance:** Nonverbal cues can reinforce or contradict what is being said, playing a critical role in how your message is received.
TIP #4: **Empathy**	**Explanation:** The ability to understand and share the feelings of others. We are living in difficult times, where life and work share the same cooking pot. As leaders, we need to be clear in our messaging, however, my most successful coaching moments have been where I was able to offer empathy and support. **Importance:** Empathy builds trust and rapport, making it easier to connect with and motivate your team.
TIP #5: **Feedback**	**Explanation:** Providing constructive responses to others' communications. Hugely important, and not one to shy away from. And don't forget to remove your emotions from your communications **Importance:** Feedback helps improve performance and fosters a culture of continuous improvement.

TIP #6: **Open-Mindedness**	**Explanation:** Being willing to listen to and consider other viewpoints. And be silent whilst doing so! We live in a very multicultural world, and it's important to learn, understand, and respect any differences. But meet in the middle. **Importance:** It encourages a collaborative environment where all team members feel valued.
TIP #7: **Confidence**	**Explanation:** Expressing your message assertively and with self-assurance. Believe in your message and role play and practice difficult ones. **Importance:** Confidence can inspire and persuade others, enhancing your leadership presence.
TIP #8: **Respect: Insert some Aretha Franklin here!**	**Explanation:** Acknowledging others' viewpoints and treating them with courtesy. **Importance:** Respectful communication fosters a positive and inclusive work environment.
TIP #9: **Adapting Your Communication Style**	**Explanation:** Modify your approach based on your audience and the context. All of my clients are different and the worst thing I can do is a broad-brush approach with them. It's never a one size fits all approach. Any one reading this have children? They all come into this world differently, with different personalities, and just like our teams, we need to cater to each one differently. **Importance:** Adaptability ensures your message is received and understood by diverse groups.

TIP #10: **Asking** **Questions**	**Explanation:** Using questions to gather information and clarify understanding. At times, my leadership clients have said, "Coach I just don't know how to approach this person with this issue". My response, "Ask questions". By doing this you gather information, you show the other person they are important, you hear their side of the situation. Open-ended questions, that don't dictate a yes or a no answer are also ones to keep in your toolbox. And preparing for a successful difficult conversation is critical, so you can plan for the outcome you would. **Importance:** Asking the right questions can lead to deeper insights and better decision-making.

SONG CHOICE

"Space Oddity" by David Bowie

This is a song that takes the listener on a journey through space and time. It tells the story of Major Tom, an astronaut who embarks on a mission to explore and contact other civilizations in the vastness of outer space.

The 7Cs Logbook

Date:

My why:

My favourite quote:

I will no longer:

I will push myself to:

Relateable movie or song:

My idol on this 'C':

How I will share it with others:

Who will hold me accountable:

2c
COMPASSION

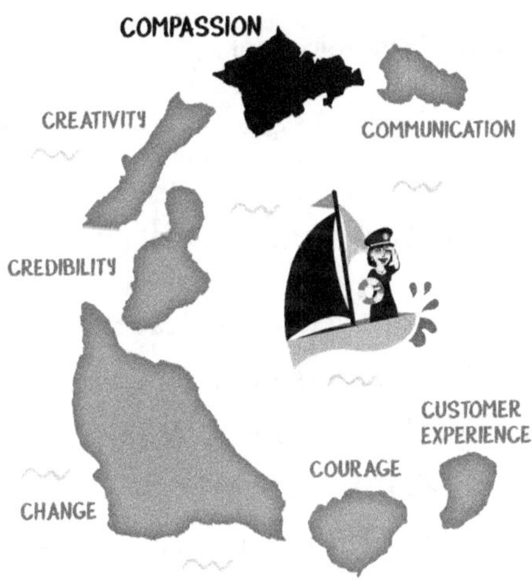

"If you want to be happy practice compassion. If you want others to be happy practice compassion."

- Dali Lama

COMPASSION CODE

- Focus on relationships
- Understand and help others and yourself
- Create psychological safe environments

Communication: A Leadership Mindset

It can be a dog-eat-dog world in leadership. Um, it is a dog-eat-dog world in leadership! I used to experience lots of stone-throwing, jibes, and other leaders finding ways to make themselves look good all the while throwing others under the bus. Not good, and from what I hear from my current leadership clients it's still happening. And if this is your style and you happen to be reading this chapter, guess what? You are not making yourself look good, in fact just worse!

The best leaders I had in corporate were extremely focused, superb at getting results, but they also had compassion and a big heart. Today, I am happy to be able to insert my fellow entrepreneurs in the category of "best leaders." Since being in business, my clients have become some of the most magnificent leaders I have ever met, and they haven't had an ounce of the expensive and ongoing leadership training provided to corporate leaders.

RELATIONSHIP SKILLS ARE KEY TO SUCCESS IN LIFE AND BUSINESS

Building healthy relationships is critical to leadership and business success. Taking a compassionate approach to this ensures great leaders suspend their judgement and appreciate others for their views and perspectives—even if they are different from their own. Having a genuine concern for the needs of others and understanding that needs change according to a person's difference is vital. To truly understand this, a successful leader will deliberately develop their emotional intelligence. This in turn will help develop positive relationships based on trust and mutual respect. Both are strong foundations and part of a commitment which, in turn, boosts morale. When the team trust their leader, they are more likely to express ideas, share concerns, and be more comfortable taking risks.

In another chapter we spoke about empathy. Empathy and compassion are closely related but distinct concepts:

Empathy

Definition: Empathy is the ability to understand and share the feelings of another person. It involves putting yourself in someone else's shoes and experiencing their emotions, perspectives, and experiences as if they were your own.

Focus: It centers on emotional resonance and understanding, where you connect with someone at an emotional level and acknowledge their feelings without necessarily agreeing with them.

Compassion

Definition: Compassion goes beyond empathy. It involves not only understanding another person's pain or suffering but also having a desire to alleviate it or help in some way.

Action-Oriented: Compassion motivates action to relieve suffering or improve the situation of others. It often includes acts of kindness, support, or empathy in action.

Key Differences Between Empathy and Compassion

The Focus: Empathy focuses on understanding and sharing emotions, while compassion involves a desire to alleviate suffering.

Action: Compassion typically leads to action or assistance, whereas empathy can exist without necessarily leading to action.

So, the million-dollar question is how do you balance both compassion and leadership?

Compassion for Self

It all starts with us. How can we possibly have compassion for others if we do not have it for ourselves? Or as we say now, give yourself some grace. Writing this book has been a gift to myself, as it has encouraged me to do lots of reflection on my life, career, and myself.

I was extremely hard on myself growing up. This intense self-criticism continued with me as an adult when I joined the corporate world, and it didn't leave for quite some time. You know, the voices in your head that tell you that you can't do it, why you don't deserve what you have, and then underline it all by claiming that you're no good? These are just some of the voices that taunted me. Can you relate? I'm "seeing" some nodding heads out there! And going into a corporate leadership role with those thoughts can be extremely debilitating. This internal self-judgement was not setting me up for success. But compassion is also about taking strides forward to change.

The dance world is tough, and as I reflect, a lot of the lack of compassion I had for myself stemmed from always having to prove myself as a dancer against all the other competition. And more often than not, feeling my gifts and talents in all departments were less than the talents and gifts of my competitors. It took a lot to boost my confidence.

One day I had a breakthrough. After 18 heats within a single competition in the dance category "American Rhythm," I was exhausted. My feet were covered with blisters, sweat was pouring down my face. At that point I stopped "actively" competing and I danced the last two multi dances without a care in the world. The exhaust emptied my mind to anything else but getting through, my feet and body knew the motions, but I was not mentally engaged. I just didn't care. My partner, Egor, was thrilled: this is exactly what he had been wanting from me—I was not worrying about what others thought. I was committed and had compassion for myself; I stopped being concerned about others as I was so "dog tired." I danced with skill and muscle-memory; I danced with grace. We ended up on the podium winning first place prizes in all the dances! And from that day on, I was able to chip away at the barriers that prevented me from being kinder to myself. I saw how important it was to allow myself room to fail. In my tiredness the voice simply kept telling me what I knew. The voices that night said, "it's ok."

Having compassion for myself was very freeing, and it allowed me room to become a much better leader. I was less critical on myself and in turn allowed others to show up as themselves. I had experienced what I knew was holding them back, so I was better able to help them. I would just meet them where they were at in their journey.

Being in business and in leadership is hard. Rewarding, but it is difficult especially in our current world. We need to prepare to fail, and we need to truly accept that failure is ok. Because this is how we learn. When we do this, we can dust ourselves off and start again.

Compassion for Others

Compassion is to look beyond your own pain to see the pain of others. That's leadership. We all have problems—part of being human—yet we receive mixed messages to drive for results no matter the cost. The key is to still drive for results; however, we can also do so with balancing our lives. Work and "life" are all in the big mixing bowl together. How can we get results, be compassionate, and help someone move forward from their problems?

Once I had a top sales performer on my team: he was incredible at sales, flawless. Then one day, it all started to slide. Not showing up for work, and when he did make it in, he was extremely tardy. After many a conversation, I learned this individual was struggling with alcoholism. Sigh. That explained it all. I was heading down the road to judging performance, yet they needed help. And I knew beneath his struggles, he was typically an excellent team player. I told him this, but he left the job as he felt he would be fired anyway.

Many years later, I received an e-mail from him. After attending Alcoholics Anonymous, he wrote me a very heartfelt letter saying that it was because of me he sought help. He wrote telling me he was so sorry for all the pain he caused me during our reporting relationship.

You see, compassion is truly key.

Taking Care of You

I wanted to share this piece with all of you, hoping it will encourage you. The concept of self-care is prevalent these days, and in my humble opinion, it holds profound significance. Whether you're in business, a leader, or simply working on personal growth and skills, mastering self-care can be pivotal to your success. The most successful people I work with have an iron-clad self-care routine.

Self-care involves nurturing your physical, emotional, and mental well-being. Here are some tips to integrate self-care into your daily life:

Physical Well-Being
Prioritize regular exercise, adequate sleep, and nutritious meals.

Emotional Well-Being
Practice mindfulness or meditation to reduce stress. Engage in activities that bring you joy and relaxation.

Mental Well-Being
Set boundaries to manage work-life balance effectively. Take breaks to rejuvenate your mind. And careful about the company you keep! There is such a thing as "Emotional Contagion." We become like those we hang around with the most.

Remember, despite the word "self" being in the phrase, investing in self-care is not selfish. Self-care is essential for maintaining compassion and effectiveness in your personal and professional life. It also builds resilience, which in turn will help you during those tough times.

Create a Psychological Safe Environment

Compassion extends beyond mere empathy. Compassion includes actively creating supportive and nurturing spaces for others. Compassion involves not only understanding and empathizing with others' experiences but also taking proactive steps to alleviate suffering and promote well-being. By fostering a psychologically safe environment, you demonstrate compassion when you foster an environment that is psychologically safe—one in which individuals feel respected, heard, and supported in their personal and professional growth. This approach aligns well with the broader theme of compassion as it pertains to creating positive and inclusive interpersonal dynamics.

How can you do this?

Ten Ways to Create A Safe Space for Those Who Need Compassion	
1. Encourage Open Communication	Promote open dialogue where everyone feels comfortable expressing their opinions, ideas, and concerns without hesitation.
2. Active Listening	Listen actively and empathetically to understand others' perspectives fully. This shows respect and validation for their thoughts and feelings. Even if you don't agree, it's ok to listen and not offer your unsolicited commentary and opinions.

3. Respect and Validate	Respect diverse viewpoints and validate others' contributions, even if they differ from your own. This promotes a culture of inclusivity.
4. Constructive Feedback	Provide feedback constructively, focusing on behavior and actions rather than personal attributes. Frame feedback as an opportunity for growth.
5. Embrace Diversity	Celebrate diversity and inclusivity in all forms, including different backgrounds, perspectives, and experiences.
6. Promote Trust	Build trust through consistency, transparency, and integrity in actions and decisions. Trust is foundational to feeling safe in any environment.
7. Manage Conflict Positively	Address conflicts promptly and constructively, encouraging resolution through dialogue and mutual understanding.
8. Lead by Example	Model the behaviors and attitudes you wish to see in others. Demonstrate vulnerability and authenticity to encourage others to do the same.
9. Provide Support	Offer resources for personal and professional development. This demonstrates care for individuals' well-being and growth.
10. Establish Clear Boundaries	Set clear expectations and boundaries for behavior and communication. Ensure everyone understands what is acceptable and respectful conduct.

GENDER & RACIAL BIASES AND MICROAGGRESSIONS

Gender and racial biases can lead to microaggressions which can subtly undermine psychological safety by marginalizing individuals based on their identity. These biases, often unconscious, manifest in everyday interactions and can erode trust and inclusivity. Leaders must actively promote awareness and education to mitigate these biases, fostering an environment where all members feel respected and valued.

I was always jibed at for my race, colour, and my name. People felt comfortable to say, "Oh you sound English but you're so dark. Your last name doesn't sound British. Where are you really from?" After a while that stings, like a small mosquito bite. It is called a microaggression because it seems like a small thing to be annoyed at but because it happens so frequently, it really gets under your skin. How easy is it to ignore a mosquito buzzing around your ears when you are ready for sleep? Not so "micro" then, is it? As leaders, we also need to be bold and call microaggressions out when we see them as they affect team dynamics.

USING CORRECT PRONOUNS

Respecting and using correct pronouns are crucial for creating a safe space. Misgendering individuals—using incorrect pronouns—can invalidate their identity and create discomfort or distress. Leaders should encourage open dialogue and provide training on pronoun usage to ensure everyone feels acknowledged and supported.

NAVIGATING NEW NORMS

Navigating new norms involves understanding and adapting to evolving societal expectations and practices. This includes staying informed about terminology and practices related to gender identity, cultural sensitivity, and inclusivity. By embracing diversity and actively addressing these issues, leaders and business owners can cultivate a workplace or community where everyone feels safe, heard, and valued.

CASE STUDY

COMPASSION IN THE FACE OF BIAS

The scene was set in a bustling office in the 1990s, a time when societal norms around gender, race, and sexuality were not nearly as progressive as they are today. The workplace was a microcosm of the wider world, reflecting both its diversity and its prejudices. As a leader, I was faced with a situation that would test my resolve and commitment to compassion and justice.

Opening Act: The Hidden Bullying

Our story begins with a valued team member, someone who had been through the complexities of life, including marriage and raising children. This individual's perceived sexuality became a subject of mockery and derision even behind closed leadership doors. The whispers and jokes were not subtle; they were loud enough to be heard and harmful enough to wound. It was a toxic undercurrent that polluted the workplace environment, eroding the principles of respect and inclusivity that I held dear.

In leadership meetings, the team member's personal life became a topic of derision. I found myself in a moral quagmire, often put on the spot to comment on their lifestyle. Each time, I deflected with a simple truth: "If they are doing their job, who cares?" But my words were ignored, and the ridicule continued.

Climax: The Confrontation

One fateful day, the tension increased during a leadership meeting. The jokes and comments became particularly cruel and overt. I felt a surge of frustration and determination. This was more than just workplace banter; it was bullying based on gender bias and resulting in open discrimination. It was then that I decided enough was enough.

Rising from my seat, I interrupted the meeting with a calm but firm declaration: "This behavior is unacceptable. It is wrong, and it has to stop. We are leaders, and our job is to create a safe and respectful environment for everyone. This person deserves our respect and support, not our judgment and ridicule."

The room fell silent. My words hung in the air, a stark contrast to the previous laughter. I could see the shock on their faces, but I also saw a flicker of realization. By calling out the behavior, I had held up a mirror to their actions, forcing them to confront the impact of their words.

Resolution: The Aftermath

In the immediate aftermath, there was an uncomfortable tension. I was unsure if the lesson had truly been learned, but I knew that I had done the right thing. Standing up for this team member was not just about defending one person; it was about setting a standard for the entire workplace.

The overt bullying ceased. The leadership team became more mindful of their words and actions, though microaggressions still lingered, a situation that would have ended quicker today. I have heard of similar situations which in our modern times have resulted in legal action and a great financial penalty to the company and individual bullies. It was a reminder that change is often slow and incremental, but it begins with a single act of courage and compassion.

Reflection: The Ongoing Battle

Fast forward to today, and the workplace has evolved, but microaggressions and biases still exist. As leaders, it is our duty to remain vigilant and vocal. The lessons from the 1990s are still relevant: if you see something, say something. Compassion in leadership is not just about being kind; it is about being prudent enough to stand up against injustice and create an environment where everyone can thrive. Otherwise, it can cause erode trust and, in the longer term, lead to serious damage to the reputation and finances of the company.

This case study serves as a reminder that leadership is not just about managing tasks but about nurturing a culture of respect and empathy. It is a delicate balance, but one that is essential for true leadership and the well-being of each member of our teams.

COACHING MOMENT

I love having the "are you okay" conversation. This is a great icebreaker to open the door when you think something might be not ok with your employee.

Instead of launching into a "your performance has dropped, what is happening" chat, instead ask the employee to open up by asking questions that invite a deeper conversation about how "life" may be impacting their ability to be all they can be at work.

SONG CHOICE

"Lean on Me" by Bill Withers

This classic song reminds us of the importance of compassion and empathy, and how we can lean on each other for support.

Date:

My why:

My favourite quote:

I will no longer:

I will push myself to:

Relateable movie or song:

My idol on this 'C':

How I will share it with others:

Who will hold me accountable:

3c
CREATIVITY

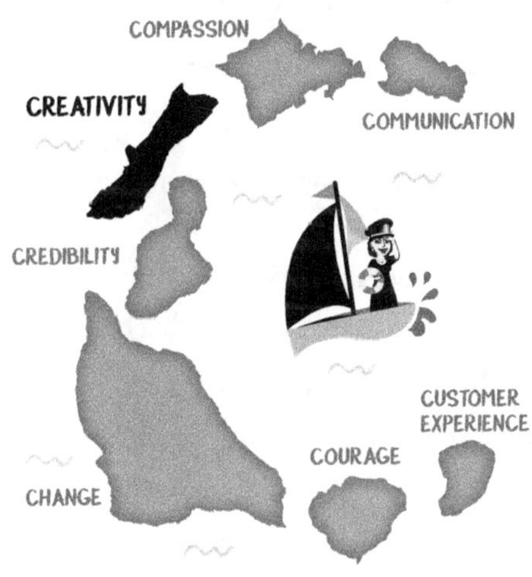

"Creativity is seeing what everyone else has seen, and thinking what no one else has thought."

- Albert Einstein

CREATIVITY CODE
- Think outside the box
- Encourage experimentation
- Foster collaboration

Unleashing Your Creative Power as a Leader

I really don't consider myself to be creative in the sense of taking an idea and coming up with a unique way of quickly executing it. I raised this question with several clients who felt the same. I am much better at executing based on the processes I've created over my career. However, if you give me a creative project—such as "find a way to make our brand align with teenagers"—with a clear outline, I can surely pull it off. But coming up with original ideas has always been a challenge for me.

Thus, when I first started my business, being creative and how it applies to me and how I work within my business was a tough concept for me to grasp. Creativity typically becomes important when considering branding, product design, marketing strategies, and social media campaigns. I needed to add creativity to my toolset when I started as I needed to find unique ways to stand out from all the other coaches. So, what did I do? What do you do when faced with a problem for which you don't have the answers? I know what I am good at and that is where I should focus my energies, so my solution was to find others with the skills I lacked. To delegate. I knew there were far better leaders out there who could help me. One such visionary is my super fabulous, Egor. He is the person behind my branding; he helped me through his creativity. Now with his help I am able to stand out in a sea of other coaches.

Hire for your weaknesses, I say!

Growing My Reach Through Empowering My Team

I then enlisted a coach, a social media expert, and a graphic designer—all leaders in their fields. This allowed me to focus on what I love: culture and people, stemming from my corporate days. As a leader, you know as well as I do that we must always find creative ways to motivate our teams. This is the type of creativity I find easier. Repeating the same methods over and over will yield the same results. And I've found I've had great results by creating events where I celebrate my staff and my clients. I host at least two such events a year: one in the summer and one around Christmas time. I provide lovely gifts for those who have supported me—

swag bags for attendees which have included branded clothing and many other items. My creative way of giving to my team and to clients has them staying with me for years.

When working with the bank years before I became an entrepreneur, I learned how to use creativity to motivate people and to improve the company culture. At the bank, we found that a culture of petty complaints was sapping energy. People tended to be quick to repeat and encourage negativity and we wanted to encourage solutions rather than dwelling on problems. I created a forum we called "You Asked, We Answered." So rather than having people moan about the quality of toilet paper, for example, or why they were not immediately granted their birthdays as holiday, they had a spot to place their questions knowing the management team (mainly me) would actually respond to their notes. The notes were collected physically, as penned notes put in a physical box, as well to a spot online. Then I would respond, sometimes the responses were online, sometimes in Town Hall types of meetings. We wanted to contain the negativity by airing issues and responding in public.

The leader's job is not to be the only source of ideas but also to encourage and champion ideas. Leaders must tap the imagination of employees at all ranks and ask inspiring questions. They also need to help their organizations to incorporate diverse perspectives, which spur creative insights, and facilitate creative collaboration. And don't forget to include your newest employees: most of the time they foster the best ideas from their recent past experiences.

Generating Ideas

Creativity is about "thinking outside of the box." And what does that mean? It means to think of novel ideas rather than use established ways of doing things. For example, in my industry, coaches get leads through flyers and mailers. I decided to try something new as if you use standard methods, you find your marketplace is crowded because your competitors are relying on the same tools. As a result, you could end up scrambling over the same clients. Instead, I chose to go out and meet people, to network. I remember when I had my first vendor table, there were many doubters. "How are you going to sell coaching at a table amongst jewelry and perfumes?" I was asked. Just watch, I said. And through making these connections and by aligning closely with a networking leader in my area, I built my business.

When I want to generate more ideas, I got to my team. During the times where I felt I lacked creativity and was not sure how to drive a particular new goal or initiative, I would huddle around with my amazing team and say, okay, let's put our heads together. And let's figure out some solutions. That way I am showing my leadership skills in identifying where we need to change and then by empowering the team to carry it out. The team to come up with their own ideas and solutions. More often than not, when we then decided on a strategy, team members would get the results they were looking for because the ideas were not mine. I was merely there to help them and encourage execute them. Surround yourself with a team that brings diverse experiences and viewpoints. This variety can spark innovative ideas that you might not come up with on your own.

Every day, we're exposed to fresh expressions of creativity, particularly in our current world of Artificial Intelligence. Just yesterday on Instagram, I noticed a subtle yet effective change: they've rounded the corners of some text elements. For example, when you click on a location, the new design looks much more appealing than before. Why make such changes? It's essential to keep moving forward with technology to stay relevant and engaging.

GETTING IDEAS FROM CRUISING AND HOLLYWOOD

I love cruising. I have noticed that every cruise ship that I have been on is looking to improve, thus the next time you travel with that cruise line, you'll find they have a larger ship with a bigger buffet and more chairs and more pools and more slides. The creativity is enormous in the cruise ship families. They are all there to compete and outdo one another quite exquisitely. If I might say insert a shout-out here to Royal Caribbean who know how to do it the right way. As I spoke about in another chapter, Disney remains first class in creativity at their parks. And continually pushes the boundaries of creativity to enhance their magic.

In a world where imagination knows no bounds and innovation reigns supreme as a leader, your ability to harness the power of creativity can set you apart, driving your team or business to new heights. How do you tap into your creative potential and inspire those around you to do the same? I found a great example in a Hollywood classic.

In the movie Castaway, one of superpowers of the character Tom Hanks plays is his creativity. Traditional ways of leaving the island were not open to him. He couldn't just book a ticket on a passing ship or charter a jet. His plan to escape the island required him to consider ideas and methods that he had never used in his days as a systems analyst with FedEx. By picturing what success would look and feel like, he was able to come up with creative solutions. His ultimate goal remained the same: to lead himself and Wilson off the island for good.

Consider Your Vision

Now imagine yourself as a visionary artist, painting a masterpiece with the strokes of your ideas and the colours of your imagination. As a creative leader, you have the power to envision the future and inspire others to join you on your creative journey. The work I do with leaders and business owners is to help them to reach into themselves to find unique solutions to whatever dilemmas come up at work.

In my line of work, I have worked with so many businesses and executives; each combination created its own mix of good luck and challenges to think and strategize your way out of. That unique way of running a business is a secret sauce with some common ingredients to which you must find ways to make it differ in the best way for your company.

For example, when Egor created my brand and named my company "The Pink Coach." I was unsure. But of course, his talent and creativity in the name and brand were spot on. He said it will make people ask, "who is the Pink Coach?" and give me a chance to showcase my business and what I do. Genius. To this day I get asked "so what do you do again?"

For some leaders this would be a problem. For me, the question gives me an opportunity to tailor what I do for the person I am speaking with, allowing me to find creative links to their business and my services. My brand suggests approachability, professionalism, and down-to-earth solutions without industry jargon and fluff., which was part of the plan.

As a leader, it's your role to create a culture where team members feel empowered to take risks and explore new ideas. As a leader, you have a variety of tools at your disposal to inspire innovation, including brainstorming sessions, design thinking workshops, and cross-functional collaboration with other teams and leaders. One of the things I enjoy leading business owners with is collaboration and the sharing of ideas. Many minds are better than one. My clients are very close and will turn to each other for help when they are stuck with being creative. It's magic to watch. Even those who are in the same industry will share their best practices of what has worked for them. I also belonged to a mastermind group for many years, and during my creativity-frozen moments, they were all there for me with their fantastic ideas.

Creativity thrives on change and to be successful we must continue to learn and move forward. As a leader, it's important to embrace change as an opportunity for growth and innovation. By fostering a mindset that welcomes change, you can inspire your team to adapt, evolve, and create. The heart of creativity is not just about creating something new; it's about creating something meaningful. As a leader, your creativity should be driven by a sense of purpose—a desire to make a positive impact on your team, organization, and the world.

Pretty deep stuff!

CASE STUDY

During my early corporate days, we often had work outings, and it was not uncommon to see some senior leaders out of control, drunk, and stumbling around. At the time, it was undeniably hilarious! Reflecting on it some 20-plus years later, the aftermath back at the office on Monday was always interesting to observe. I watched as these same leaders engaged in awkward conversations at the coffee station, having committed what we called a CLM—a Career Limiting Move.

I observed leaders like John, the VP of Sales, and Lisa, the Marketing Director, trying to navigate the aftermath of their weekend escapades. Their reputations were tarnished, and the respect they once commanded was eroding. During this encounter, I had to issue a performance letter on breach of code of conduct due to events that were fueling gossip after the event. It was a tough lesson for me to deliver, however, sending a strong message was critical.

What do you think happened? The lesson was clear: to be a leader, you need to act like one, all the time. Leadership is a way of life, not something you can turn on and off at your convenience. The behavior of these leaders during those outings eroded their credibility and respect, impacting their ability to lead effectively. True leadership demands consistency, integrity, and professionalism, both inside and outside the workplace. It's about setting an example at all times, as your actions are always being observed and judged by those you lead.

Fast forward several years, and I found myself coaching Mark, a business leader who had built quite a successful business. We met in his elegant, glass-walled office, overlooking the city's skyline. Mark was charismatic and well-liked, but as our coaching relationship developed, it became clear that there were no social boundaries between him and his clients. Professional meetings often turned into social gatherings, blurring the lines and muddying the waters of his professional relationships.

One afternoon, we sat down in the boardroom, a spacious, minimalist room with a large oak table and plush chairs. The sunlight streamed in, casting long shadows on the table as we discussed his situation. I could see the realization dawning on him as we talked about the importance of 'professional boundaries.' Mark had an 'ah-ha' moment when he recognized that his lack of boundaries was eroding his credibility and the respect of his clients.

Mark and I developed a strategy to turn things around. He made the difficult decision to separate business activities from social ones and draw a clear line between them. He communicated this change to his clients, explaining the need for a more professional approach. It wasn't easy, and Mark did lose some clients who were more interested in the social aspect than the business. However, this was a necessary step to clean his closet (thanks, Judi) and make room for new, better-fitting opportunities.

Over the next few months, we held regular sessions in the boardroom to monitor his progress. Mark started to regain his credibility as he demonstrated consistency, reliability, and professionalism. His clients began to see him in a new light, respecting him as a true leader who could be trusted in all settings.

In conclusion, the actions of leaders are always under scrutiny, both in and out of the workplace. The experiences of John, Lisa, and Mark underscore the importance of maintaining credibility through consistent, professional behavior. For Mark, the journey to regain credibility was challenging but ultimately rewarding, as he rebuilt his reputation and established a clear boundary between his professional and social lives. Leadership is a continuous journey of self-awareness, integrity, and the unwavering commitment to set the right example at all times.

COACHING MOMENT

How do you currently foster creativity within your team or organization, and what changes could you make to further enhance this environment?

Can you think of a problem you recently faced that required a creative solution? How did you approach it, and what was the outcome?

In what ways can embracing failure and taking risks lead to more creative outcomes in your work or leadership style?

SONG CHOICE

"Imagine" by John Lennon

The lyrics encourage thinking beyond conventional boundaries and envisioning a world of possibilities, making it an inspiring anthem for creativity and innovation.

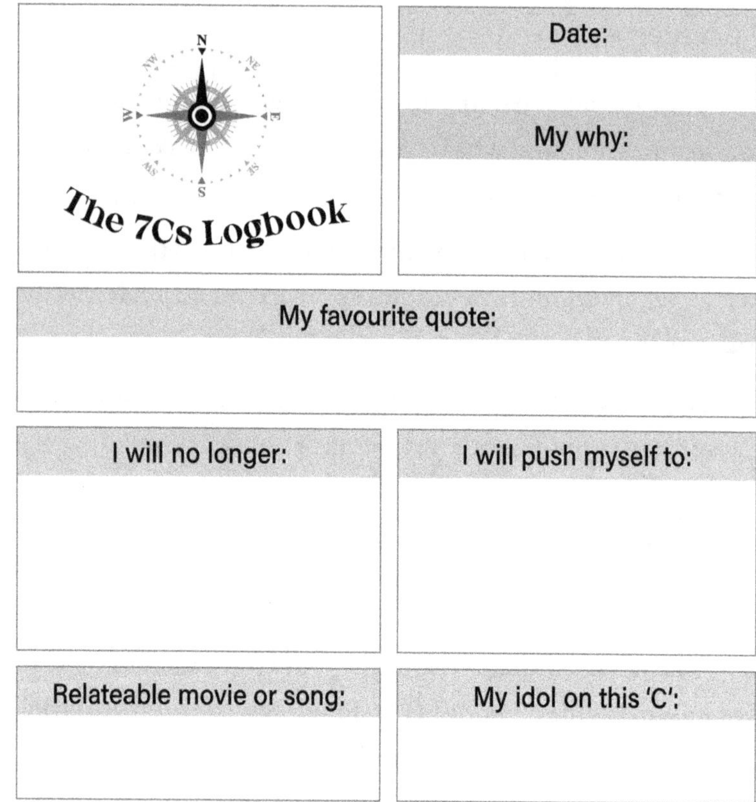
The 7Cs Logbook
Date:
My why:
My favourite quote:
I will no longer:
I will push myself to:
Relateable movie or song:
My idol on this 'C':
How I will share it with others:
Who will hold me accountable:

4c
CREDIBILITY

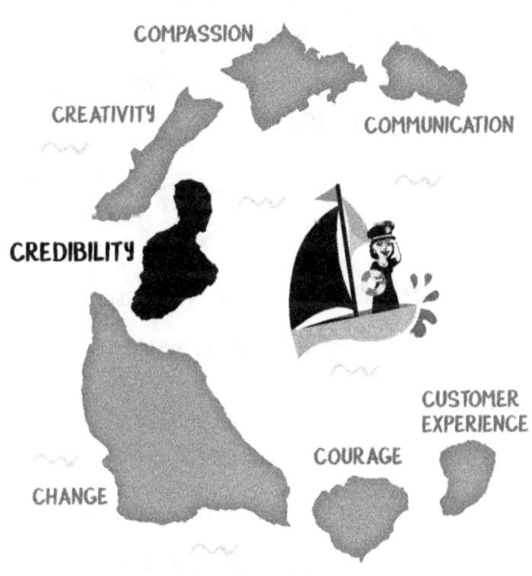

"You gotta own it and lead it."

- Coach Judi Hughes

CREDIBILITY CODE

- Be a real person who is transparent, trustworthy, and talented
- Value feedback, recognize and appreciate your team
- Lead by example, be professional and communicate

Credibility is the foundation of effective leadership. It is built through consistent actions, transparent communication, ethical behavior, and a commitment to continuous improvement. Leaders who prioritize credibility inspire trust, foster loyalty, and drive their teams to achieve remarkable success. One of my first lessons in leadership is that teams will respect leaders who can acknowledge their errors and take responsibility for them. It's a sign of credibility and maturity. Moreover, by learning from your mistakes and sharing those lessons with others, you can prevent similar errors in the future and foster a culture of continuous improvement.

When I was only 23 years old, a seasoned leader once told me "You don't need to know everything, you just know where to find the answers". That is advice that I follow to this day. I would rather you say, let me take that away and get back to you on that, than reply with something you made up on the spot which turns out to be incorrect. Imagine how you will be perceived if you give an incorrect response to look more credible and your team ends up taking action based on your ego-saving, incorrect statement. Be honest and you'll appear truthful, authentic, and credible.

Building in Safety Through Testing Ideas

One thing I love doing with my clients is to help them to "see around their corners." By this I mean we do an exercise which illuminates their blind spots and provides creative solutions to their business and leadership problems. The success of this exercise has given me credibility as a leader. And it has taken over 25 years of practice to hone my craft. It is by sharing our vulnerability and not pretending to be perfect that we attract the most respect.

I learned about the concept of "fail-safe" in the business industry. This is a concept in which a system is designed to automatically reroute to the safest actions, or to adjust, when threatening circumstances pop up to prevent total failure. Essentially, a fail-safe system is built to continue functioning even when one or more of its components fail. This principle became especially relevant when the pandemic hit the world in 2020, catching most of us unprepared for such a widespread and disruptive event.

Considering this, how can you, as a leader, create credibility by ensuring you have robust plans in place for your business or team? What is a fail-safe system for your business? The key lies in meticulous preparation for inevitable setbacks. It's not a matter of if something will go wrong, but when it will. Therefore, developing a comprehensive strategy that anticipates potential failures and outlines clear, actionable responses is crucial. This foresight not only enhances your leadership credibility but also significantly strengthens the resilience of your business, enabling it to weather unforeseen challenges effectively.

Consider the fail-safe systems in various industries. In aviation, for instance, airplanes are designed with multiple redundant systems to ensure that if one fails, others can take over to maintain safety. In technology, data centers often have backup power supplies and duplicate servers to prevent downtime during power outages or hardware failures. These examples illustrate the importance of anticipating possible points of failure and creating contingency plans that allow operations to continue smoothly despite disruptions.

As a leader, adopting a fail-safe mindset means investing time and resources into risk assessment and mitigation. This involves identifying potential vulnerabilities in your operations and developing protocols to address them swiftly and efficiently. Additionally, it requires cultivating a culture of adaptability and resilience within your team, encouraging them to think proactively about solutions and remain flexible in the face of change.

When the pandemic struck, those businesses and leaders who had fail-safe mechanisms in place were better equipped to adapt to the sudden shifts in the market and operational landscape. They could pivot their strategies, leverage technology for remote work, and continue serving their customers despite the challenges. This adaptability not only ensured their survival but also reinforced their credibility and reliability in the eyes of their stakeholders.

Preparing for failure by implementing fail-safe systems and strategies is not just a technical necessity but a hallmark of effective leadership. By anticipating challenges and equipping your business with the tools and mindset to handle them, you demonstrate foresight, responsibility, and a commitment to maintaining stability and continuity. This proactive approach will ultimately set you apart as a credible leader capable of steering your team through both calm and turbulent times

Diversity in one's thoughts and a growth mindset always lead to creativity—you just need to set aside time to think! Consider how you can actively encourage and inspire creativity within your teams. Perhaps a reward system for innovative ideas, or an innovation award. Don't forget to include your new team members when brainstorming. Often, they come with hidden experience, and we need to encourage their creativity in the early days of their employment.

Build Trust Through Authenticity

Authenticity is your superpower. It's about being true to yourself and your values, even when the going gets tough. Share your stories, be vulnerable, and connect with others on a human level. Back in the day, I had a fear of being vulnerable, worrying if this would be seen as a weakness. Well, it's quite the opposite.

I was at a networking event this week, where three speakers shared vulnerable stories, accidents of loved ones, loss, and mental health issues. And everyone was captivated. People trust those who are genuine. Authenticity is about being transparent and honest in your interactions. It's about admitting when you don't know something and being open to learning from others. Authentic leaders inspire trust because they are real – they don't pretend to be someone they're not. They are comfortable in their skin and are not afraid to show their true selves to the world. They are credible!

"TMI" – Too Much Information

But then there are also leaders who make the error of sharing too much. I often see business owners "air their dirty laundry" all over social media platforms. I do believe in sharing some strategic life moments, but we need to be cautious that we don't overshare. So many times, I have heard whispers in the entrepreneur community about someone posting about something bad going on in the world, the war, or commenting on a political matter.

In my view, we need to be super careful here. Again, is this the platform to showcase and rant about what is going on in the world? You might be surprised at how many people avoid doing business with individuals who overshare on social media. Again, to remain a credible leader, you must consider the professional ramifications of whatever you share. Engaging in certain conflicts or arguments may bring you down to a level where it's difficult to stay out of unintended arguments. While others might enjoy the chaos, you may end up feeling some negative consequences to your credibility.

As much as you may feel that sharing your opinions is part of your credibility, never forget context—the environment in which you are sharing your message and the audience that will see it. If you choose to share views that may be contentious, how can you do so in a non-confrontational way? Maybe the information you are making public is best shared between friends or in a private setting. Keeping your mouth at times is the best strategic choice. You may think that to be "real" you have to say everything on your mind, but as a leader, it is also your job to prioritize harmony, professional integrity, and even personal safety. It may feel difficult to stay silent about some discussions going viral online. It may feel difficult to balance authenticity and credibility. When you are in doubt, consider that there are many ways to be true to oneself without necessarily sharing every opinion and every personal thing that happens to you on social media. As a leader, this will have to be a conscious choice as sharing things that drag you into a fight can limit your ability to lead—and could harm you later in your career.

Managing Change and Staying Credible

Every day I spend as a business leader, I need to be creative. Business is not linear. My clients need to move with the ever-changing landscape, which means I need also need to be able to move quickly to stay ahead of the game. What does that mean for you? What do you need to implement to be more creative and stay credible with what is happening in your industry?

What course should you take, or what mentorship should you seek? Remember, leadership is all about positive influence, and you must continually strive to improve!

Credibility is key in leadership. Your actions and decisions shape how others perceive you. It's not just about being knowledgeable; it's about being reliable, trustworthy, and authentic. When you demonstrate creativity and adaptability, you show that you are proactive and forward-thinking. This builds trust with your clients and team.

Consistency and Credibility

Leaders must be ready to change based on "an ever-changing landscape" yet must also not change? How can both be possible? It is true that leaders who demonstrate a consistent approach to actions, decisions, and behavior are more likely to be trusted. Imagine a brand that keeps changing its logo or a leader whose values shift with the wind. These are areas where consistency shows and where it breeds trust.

Consistency and integrity pair well together. Integrity is about doing the right thing, even when it's not an easy thing. It's about being honest and ethical in all your dealings, both personally and professionally. Integrity builds trust and credibility with your team and your stakeholders as when you have a decision to make it means those who know and trust your brand can have an understanding of how you will act. This is a form of consistency that means you act in a way that illuminates your respect for your values and principles, even in the face of adversity.

Be consistent in your actions, your words, and your values. Consistency means delivering on your promises, day in and day out. It means being reliable and dependable – someone others can count on. Consistency is about building a reputation for excellence and maintaining it over time. Consistent leaders are predictable in the best possible way—they are consistent in their behavior and their decision-making, which builds trust and credibility with their team.

BACK UP YOUR CONSISTENCY WITH EXPERTISE

Become the go-to person in your field, the one everyone turns to for advice. Dive deep into your subject, stay updated with the latest trends, and never stop learning. Your knowledge will be your greatest asset. Attend conferences, read books, take courses – whatever it takes to stay ahead of the curve. Expertise isn't just about what you know; it's also about how you apply that knowledge. Share your insights, write articles, and give presentations – become a thought leader in your industry. Your expertise will not only earn you respect but also inspire confidence in those around you. In my early days of business, I knew one of my strong suits was sales.

During a trip to Mexico, I observed a beach vendor selling bags without even talking! It was amazing to see. On my plane ride home, I wrote my first workshop: "How to Sell Like a Beach Vendor", sales training for entrepreneurs. Right then and there, I established my credibility in sales, and every class I offered sold out. Ten years later, I am still known for my expertise in this field and my excellence in coaching sales.

CONSISTENTLY SHOW YOU VALUE YOUR TEAM

Feedback is a gift, even when it's tough to hear. Seek feedback from colleagues, mentors, and even critics. Use it to improve, grow, and become the best leader you can be. Feedback is essential for personal and professional growth. It provides valuable insights into your strengths and weaknesses and helps you identify areas for improvement. Seek feedback from those you trust and respect and be open to receiving both positive and negative feedback. Act on the feedback you receive – use it to make meaningful changes in your behavior and your leadership style. Feedback is a continuous process—seek it regularly and use it to continuously improve and evolve as a leader.

Show you need and value others as it takes a credible leader needs a team. Catch people doing things well. Always be on the lookout for great work and don't wait to recognize excellent work. How amazing would it feel if your leader called you to one side and privately and quickly praised what they have just witnessed?

Some people prefer public recognition and others prefer to be rewarded quietly – know your team and how they're likely to respond to recognition and reward. Develop a culture of recognition where it becomes the norm to congratulate people and be respectful of feedback.

Inspire Others to Credible Leadership Through Your Actions

Actions speak louder than words. Lead by example, and inspire others with your work ethic, your passion, and your commitment. Be the kind of leader you would follow. Leadership is not just about giving orders; it's about setting an example for others to follow. Inspire your team with your actions – show them what's possible when you work hard, stay committed, and never give up. Be a role model for your team – someone they can look up to and emulate. Your actions have the power to motivate and inspire others to be their best selves. This approach not only builds credibility but also fosters a culture of continuous improvement and resilience.

CASE STUDY

During my early corporate days, we often had work outings, and it was not uncommon to see some senior leaders out-of-control drunk, stumbling around and slurring their words. At the time, it was undeniably hilarious. Back at the office on Monday after these events was always as interesting. I watched as these same leaders engaged in awkward conversations at the coffee station, trying to recover their credibility after having committed what we called CLMs—Career Limiting Moves. Their reputations were tarnished, the respect they once commanded eroding. After one such weekend, I had to issue a performance letter for someone's breach of code of conduct. It was a tough lesson for me to deliver, however, sending a strong message was critical.

The lesson is clear: to be a leader, you need to act like one, all of the time. Leadership is a way of life, not something you can turn on and off at your convenience. The behavior of these leaders during those outings eroded their credibility and respect, impacting their ability to lead effectively. True leadership demands consistency, integrity, and professionalism, both inside and outside the workplace. It's about setting an example at all times, as your actions are always being observed and judged by those you lead.

Fast forward several years, and I found myself coaching a business leader who had built quite a successful business in real estate. We met in their elegant, glass-walled office, overlooking the city's skyline. They were charismatic and well-liked, but as our coaching relationship developed, it became clear that there were no social boundaries between them and their clients. Professional meetings often turned into social gatherings, blurring the lines and muddying the waters of professional relationships.

One afternoon, we sat down in the boardroom, a spacious, minimalist room with a large oak table and plush chairs. The sunlight streamed in, casting long shadows on the table as we discussed the situation. I could see the realization dawning on them as we talked about the importance of "professional boundaries." I could see the "ah-ha" moment as the realization sunk in right on their face. They recognized that lack of boundaries was eroding their credibility and the respect of their clients.

Together we developed a strategy to turn things around. They made the difficult decision to separate business activities from social ones and draw a clear line between them and communicated this change to clients. It wasn't easy, and they did lose some clients who were more interested in the social aspect than the business.

However, this was a necessary step to clean up and make room for new, better-fitting opportunities.

Over the next few months, we held regular sessions in the boardroom to monitor progress. As they demonstrated consistency, reliability, and professionalism their clients began to see them in a new light, respecting them as a true leader who could be trusted in all settings.

In conclusion, the actions of leaders are always under scrutiny, both in and out of the workplace. The journey to regain credibility was challenging but ultimately rewarding, it is possible to rebuild a tarnished reputation. Leadership is a continuous journey of self-awareness, integrity, and the unwavering commitment to always set the right example.

COACHING MOMENT

How do you think you are perceived as a leader? Are your actions consistent with the values and standards you promote? Is there room for growth or improvement, and what does that look like? Reflect on the image you project and consider if it aligns with your vision of effective leadership.

What steps can you take to ensure you are always acting in a way that builds trust and respect? Are there areas where you might be falling short or could benefit from feedback? Leadership is an ongoing journey of self-improvement. I encourage all of us to continue to look in the mirror often and see where we need to adjust our leadership behaviors. By doing so, we not only enhance our credibility but also inspire those around us to strive for excellence.

Remain mindful of the importance of maintaining credibility through consistent, ethical, and professional conduct. Consider what I call table stakes, the simple things, like arriving on time. Responding to e mails, questions, and messages in a timely fashion. This ongoing journey of self-improvement not only enhances our leadership effectiveness but also inspires those around us to pursue excellence.

SONG CHOICE

"Man in the Mirror" by Michael Jackson

This song shows self-reflection and accountability. Jackson sings about being aware of making errors and displays vulnerability through such acknowledgements. Through his song, he demonstrates credibility; his courage in being willing to change to be a better leader is reflected in the title of the song.

Date:

My why:

My favourite quote:

I will no longer:

I will push myself to:

Relateable movie or song:

My idol on this 'C':

How I will share it with others:

Who will hold me accountable:

5c
CHANGE

"Change is hard at first, messy in the middle, but gorgeous at the end."

\- Robin Sharma

CHANGE CODE

- Adapt quickly
- Embrace uncertainty
- Lead by example

I think this quote sums it up in a couple of sentences why we stay comfortable with the status quo as human beings. Because change is hard. However, strong leaders embrace change. They embrace the challenge that change gives them.

Why change? When we change ourselves, circumstances, and processes, then the magic happens. Growth doesn't happen when we stay within the comfort zone of the box. It happens when we take risks and embrace change. Ask yourself, when did you last experience growth? Was it during the easy-going times, or was it during the tough times that you grew and learned your growth lessons?

For me, a huge change in my life was immigrating to Canada. It was a change in land, relationships, and culture, and I made these large changes with little support and without a job to provide routine and financial support. So, I needed to do the work to adapt to my new surroundings and lifestyle.

Change is an inevitable part of life. Whether we like it or not, change is constantly happening around us, shaping our world and influencing our lives. Let's explore the concept of change, its significance, types, challenges, and strategies for managing and embracing change.

What is Change?

Change is moving from one state, condition, or phase to another. It can be gradual or sudden, planned or unplanned. Change can occur in various aspects of life, including personal, professional, social, and environmental. Change can be positive, leading to growth, innovation, and improvement, or it can be negative, causing disruption, uncertainty, and discomfort. When it is the latter, leaders must lead their teams from that negative, disruptive place through the uncertainty and discomfort to a place of improved circumstances. They do this by being innovative—with growth and improvement being the result of change.

THE SIGNIFICANCE OF CHANGE

Change is essential for progress and growth. Without change, we would remain stagnant, unable to adapt to new circumstances or seize new opportunities. Change challenges us to evolve, learn, and improve. It forces us out of our comfort zones and pushes us to discover new skills, perspectives, and possibilities. Change is a catalyst for innovation, creativity, and transformation.

TYPES OF CHANGE

Change can take many forms, including:

Organizational	Changes in the structure, culture, or processes of an organization
Personal	Changes in behavior, habits, or attitudes of individuals and ourselves, or changes that come because of health issues
Social	Changes in society's norms, values, or institutions.
Technological	Changes in technology that impact how we live, work, and communicate.
Environmental	Changes in the environment, such as climate change or natural disasters.

CHANGE IS RARELY EASY

Change will often be met with some resistance, fear, and uncertainty. People may resist change due to fear of the unknown, loss of control, or perceived threat to their status or security. Uncertainty about the future, leads to anxiety and stress. Implementing change often requires resources, such as time, money, and expertise, which may be limited and this is a large reason for the discomfort of change. Discomfort is magnified within organizations because of the larger scale of the change. The company brand and culture can impact how change is perceived and implemented. A culture that is resistant to change can hinder the change process.

STRATEGIES FOR MANAGING CHANGE

To effectively manage change, leaders will develop strategies:

Communicate Effectively

Keep your team or employees informed about the reasons for change, the process, and the expected outcomes. Address concerns and listen to feedback. Map out a change journey with timelines. It is important to share why we are doing something. Why the change? And framing it so it is clear what is in it for the each member of the team is also important.

Create a Vision

Develop a clear vision for the change and communicate it. Help team members understand how the change will benefit them and the organization. Be clear honest and transparent. Bring them into your world and vision; let them be part of the change.

Empower Employees

Involve employees in the change process and empower them to contribute ideas and solutions. Encourage collaboration and teamwork.

Provide Support

Offer support and resources to help employees navigate the change process. Provide training and development opportunities to build skills and confidence. I was once managing a team of tenured employees who were older than me. During times of change in which there were many, I would enlist the most negative person on my team and throw them a bone. I need your help, I would say. You do? Then I would give them a task and a role in the change management process so they could be the leader and help me to roll out that change. Sounds crazy, right? But it worked.

Monitor Progress

Monitor the progress of the change initiative and make adjustments as needed. Celebrate successes and learn from setbacks.

Embracing Change

Embracing change can be challenging, but it also offers opportunities for growth and development. Embracing change requires you to adapt to new circumstances. Life is full of change and through simply living life and going through all that is needed to learn to get you to a place of leadership, no doubt you've had to tap into your resilience. Embrace that change—instead of resisting it, you will need to cope with the challenges that come, perhaps through grit, and through ensuring you have the rest and resources you will need. Because you'll need your resilience to accept change as well as to manage the challenges you will experience as you lead your team through your vision.

You will need to be open to new ideas and ways of doing things. But if you have a growth mindset, you will see change as an opportunity for learning and improvement. Leaders need to stay curious in good times and bad – to always learn and grwot through staying on top of new trends and information.

Embracing Change and Taking Risks to Lead

Change is inevitable, and as a leader, your ability to navigate change and take risks can set you apart. Leaders who embrace change understand that it's not about avoiding failure, but about learning from it and using it as a stepping stone to success.

THE IMPORTANCE OF CHANGE IN LEADERSHIP

Change is a constant in today's fast-paced world. Leaders who resist change often find themselves left behind, unable to adapt to new challenges and opportunities. Embracing change allows leaders to stay ahead of the curve, innovate, and drive growth within their organizations.

TAKING RISKS AS A LEADER

Taking risks is a fundamental part of leadership. It involves stepping outside your comfort zone, trying new things, and accepting the possibility of failure. While taking risks can be daunting, it is often necessary for driving change and achieving success.

When I started my business in 2014, it was a massive risk. No clients, just a brand that Egor, my amazing design expert created, and moi. I was out pounding the pavement and networking to meet new potential leads. I remember starting my business and taking a trip, using my flying time as quiet work time (all thanks a credit to the amazing Robin Sharma for that tip). During the flight time, I mapped out my journey and what I wanted my website to look like. My journey included my huge goals and dreams and how I would get there—the majority of those goals and dreams mapped out so many years ago have come to pass. Why? Because I was bold and took risks. Was I scared? Oh yes, but with risk comes reward.

FAILSAFE STRATEGIES

While taking risks is important, it's also essential to have failsafe strategies in place. Failsafe strategies are backup plans that help minimize the impact of failure. They can include:

Risk Assessment

Before taking a risk, assess the potential impact and likelihood of success. This can help you make informed decisions and identify potential pitfalls.

Contingency Planning

Develop contingency plans for potential failures. Identify alternative approaches or solutions that can be implemented if your initial plan does not succeed.

Learning from Failure

Instead of viewing failure as a setback, see it as an opportunity to learn and grow. Analyze what went wrong and use that knowledge to improve your approach in the future.

I have failed over and over again, but this is learning that has built my resilience muscle. Plan to fail, and with that plan, you will fail safely with a plan in place. During my career, I was on many contingency plan committees, from bird flu to SARS we had a plan for it all. Fast forward to the dreaded Covid-19 pandemic, and I was able to be nimble and help my clients plan their failsafe plans and keep their businesses successful.

Change is inevitable, and as a leader, your ability to navigate change and take risks can set you apart. Leaders who embrace change understand that it's not about avoiding failure, but about learning from it and using it as a steppingstone to success.

Change is a constant in today's fast-paced world. Leaders who resist change often find themselves left behind, unable to adapt to new challenges and opportunities. Embracing change allows leaders to stay ahead of the curve, innovate, and drive growth within their organizations.

CASE STUDY

EMBRACING CHANGE - FROM EMPLOYEE TO ENTREPRENEUR

Act I: The Leap into the Unknown

Imagine this: it's 2014, and I've just decided to transition from employee to entrepreneur. It felt like diving into the deep end of the entrepreneurial pool without a life jacket. The fear was palpable, but as a woman determined to conquer the business world, I knew there was no turning back. Change was not just necessary; it was inevitable.

Act II: Navigating the Storm

The first step in my journey was to hire a coach. Not just any coach, but someone who could guide me through the tumultuous waters of entrepreneurship. This coach helped me navigate both the business side of things and the often-tricky waters of personal finance. It was a crucial decision that provided me with the support and direction I needed.

The journey was far from easy. There were moments of doubt and fear, but each challenge was a learning opportunity. I had to battle my mind and conquer my fears daily. The transition didn't happen overnight, and it certainly wasn't a walk in the park. But with determination and the right guidance, I began to see progress.

Act III: The Transformation

As I look back on my leap from employee to entrepreneur, I marvel at how far I've come. Each bump in the road, each moment of doubt, was a steppingstone to where I am today. The journey taught me resilience, adaptability, and the importance of embracing change.

Today, I use my experiences to coach others through their own transitions. Change is a constant in life and business, and managing it effectively is crucial for success. I teach my clients to embrace change, take risks, and understand that fear is a natural part of the process.

One of my clients, Emily, was struggling with the decision to leave her corporate job and start her own business. She was paralyzed by fear and uncertainty. Through our coaching sessions, I helped her to see change as an opportunity rather than a threat. By breaking down the process and tackling each challenge step by step, Emily was able to make the transition smoothly and successfully.

Another client, Mike, faced significant changes within his organization. He needed to lead his team through a major restructuring. By applying the principles of embracing change and focusing on the positives, Mike was able to guide his team through the transition, maintaining morale and productivity.

In conclusion, the journey from employee to entrepreneur taught me invaluable lessons about change. It's not easy, but with the right mindset and support, it is possible to navigate even the most daunting transitions. Embrace change, take risks, and never underestimate the power of a good coach. The journey may be long and challenging, but it's a ride worth taking.

COACHING MOMENT

Ask yourself this question: what needs to change now in your life? Work, home, you, people, places, leaders? And what will you do to get there? How will you tackle this and what plans do you need to put in place for success?

Change is a constant in life. By understanding its significance, types, challenges, and strategies for managing and embracing it, we can navigate change more effectively and embrace the opportunities it brings. Change challenges us to grow, learn, and evolve, making us more resilient, adaptable, and innovative. So, embrace change as a journey of discovery and transformation, and let it propel you toward a brighter future.

SONG CHOICE

"Ain't No Mountain High Enough"
by Marvin Gaye and Tammi Terrell

This timeless classic represents the idea that no challenge is too great to overcome, highlighting the importance of embracing change and overcoming obstacles.

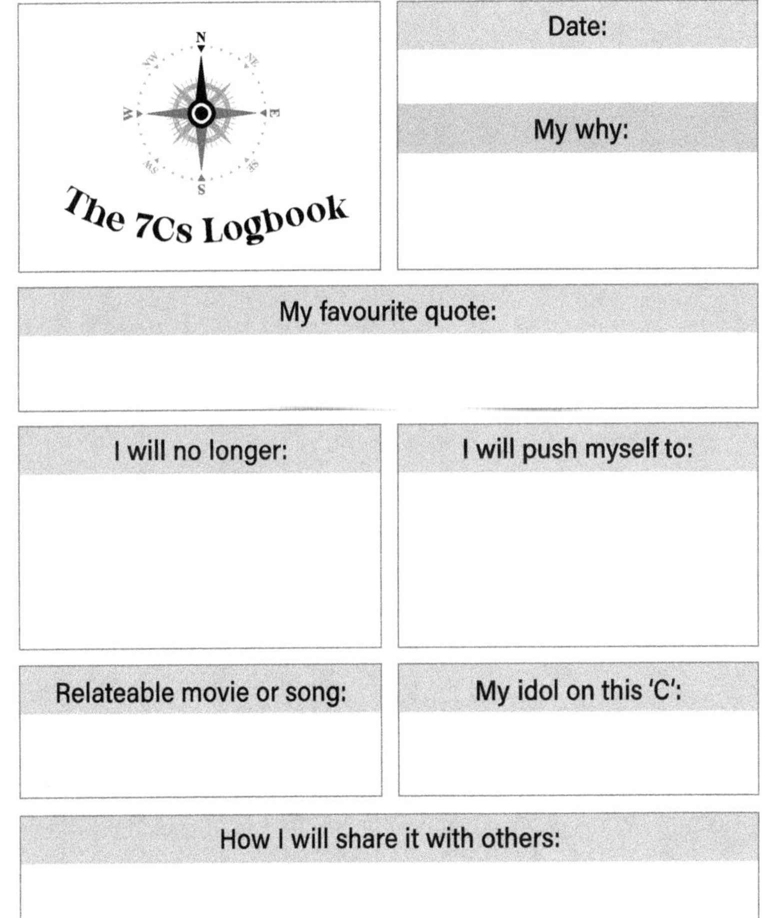
The 7Cs Logbook

Date:

My why:

My favourite quote:

I will no longer:

I will push myself to:

Relateable movie or song:

My idol on this 'C':

How I will share it with others:

Who will hold me accountable:

6c
COURAGE

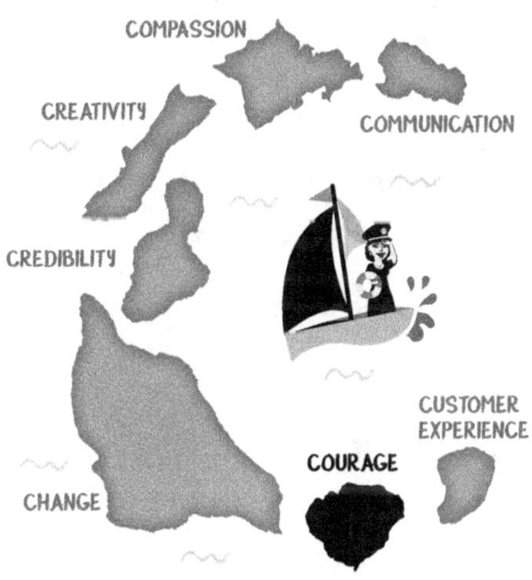

"Courage is not the absence of fear, but the triumph over it. The brave man is not he who does not feel afraid, but he who conquers that fear."

- Nelson Mandela

COURAGE CODE

- Be vulnerable
- Take calculated Risks
- Stand up for your values

My whole life I have struggled with courage. Many will be surprised to hear this.

"Really, Coach, that doesn't sound like you!"

Oh yes, it's me!

I have to say that dance was a turning point in my life, allowing me a chance to notice my fear, conquer it, and practice courage. It taught me so much about courage and leadership. Courage to try new styles, take exams, dance on stage. As my skills improved, dance gave me the opportunity to set an example as a leader to the other students. I clearly remember my lovely Monica Cleaver, owner of "Mo's Place" in Reading, England saying to me (during a painfully long show rehearsal), "Oh, look at you, Claudine! You are so responsible, and showing what it is like to be patient during all of this. Well done." Me being a leader at the age of 13. To this day, she continues to inspire me with her leadership and sass! And she continues to be one of my entrepreneurial role models.

Alyson is another who I think of with reverence. She was an amazing leader who mentored me early in my career during my time at the bank. She saw something in me and took a chance: she promoted me to a leadership role before I felt ready to step up to that stage in my career. I was petrified. I was young and inexperienced but prepared to try anything. Alyson was my first coach and mentor. I heeded her advice well, doing everything she suggested during our coaching sessions. I believe she completely set me up for success in my role. She had loads of courage and experience, and I wanted every piece of that!

Alyson would role-play challenging conversations I had to hold with my team. "Always explain the 'why,' Claudine," she'd remind me. She helped me to find the courage I didn't have by pushing me to step as a leader outside of my comfort zone, because magic never happens when you stay inside of it.

In 2014, I started my entrepreneurial journey, and once again I found myself feeling scared. I had to dig deep into my courage toolbox to get things started. As I say to my clients, if it was easy everyone would do it. Being in business takes courage. A whole heap of it.

For me, leadership is a way of life, something we choose to do all day and every day. Once we choose the leadership path and show up like a leader, there is some kind of magic in it. How you walk, talk, dress, and interact = leadership = courage. Courage, like leadership, is a journey. What can you do to work on enhancing both?

Courage is not just about facing your fears head-on; it's about embracing them, dancing with them, and turning them into your greatest allies. As a leader, courage is your secret weapon, your superpower that propels you to greatness and inspires others to follow in your footsteps.

Imagine courage in this way: You're standing at the edge of a cliff, ready to take a leap into the unknown. That's courage! It's about taking risks, stepping outside of your comfort zone, and embracing the adventure that lies ahead. It's about being bold, being brave, and being willing to fail in pursuit of your dreams.

Courage is not always about big, bold actions. Sometimes, it's about the small, everyday acts of bravery that make a big difference. It's about speaking up when others stay silent, taking the lead when others hesitate, and standing firm in your convictions when others waver. As a leader, courage is your compass, guiding you through the challenges and uncertainties of the leadership journey. It's what gives you the strength to face adversity, the resilience to bounce back from failure, and the vision to see opportunities where others see obstacles.

But courage is not just for you; it's also for those you lead. Your courage is contagious: it inspires and empowers others to be courageous in their own lives and work. By establishing courage as a desirable value in your company, you create a culture of bravery, where people are encouraged to take risks, think creatively, and push the boundaries of what's possible.

So, how can you cultivate courage as a leader? It starts with self-awareness – knowing your strengths, your weaknesses, and your fears. It's about being honest with yourself and with others. It is about being open and vulnerable in front of yourself and your team—being willing to admit dread, anxiety, and uncertainty because doing so is truthful even though you may fear you'll come across as weak to some team members. It's also about surrounding yourself with a team of diverse talents and perspectives, who can support you and challenge you to grow. You will create a tighter team as being honest while displaying courage leads to trust.

Courageous leadership is not always easy, but it is always worth it. It's about being true to yourself, your values, and your vision, even when it's hard. It's about leading with your heart, your head, and your gut, and inspiring others to do the same.

Embrace Your Inner Superhero

Think of yourself as a superhero on a mission to save the day! Identify your unique superpowers – your strengths, skills, and talents – and use them to lead with confidence and courage. Visualize yourself donning your superhero cape, ready to take on any challenge that comes your way. Remember, every great leader has a bit of superhero in them – it's what sets you apart and inspires others to follow your lead.

Here's how you do it:

STEP INTO THE SPOTLIGHT

Imagine yourself on a stage, with all eyes on you. Take a deep breath, stand tall, and speak up! Don't be afraid to share your ideas, voice your opinions, and take the lead in challenging situations. Your voice matters, and your perspective is valuable. Step into the spotlight with confidence, knowing that you have the power to make a difference and inspire others to do the same.

CHANNEL YOUR INNER MAVERICK

In the movie Top Gun, Tom Cruise's character, Maverick, dared to be different and courageous. Like Maverick, I encourage you to break free from the status quo and dare to be different! Take calculated risks, think outside the box, and challenge conventional thinking. Be bold, be brave, and blaze your own trail. Remember, it's the mavericks who change the world – those who are unafraid to challenge the norm and pursue their vision with passion and purpose.

CONQUER YOUR FEARS

Make a list of your fears, big and small. Then, tackle them one-by-one, starting with the smallest ones. Each time you conquer a fear, celebrate your victory and build momentum for the next challenge. Remember, courage is not the absence of fear but the willingness to act in spite of it. By facing your fears, you'll become stronger, more resilient, and more confident in your abilities.

CULTIVATE A CULTURE OF COURAGE

Lead by example and inspire your team to be courageous. Encourage them to take risks, share their ideas, and challenge the status quo. Create a safe space where failure is seen as a stepping-stone to success. By fostering a culture of courage, you'll create a team that is innovative, resilient, and unafraid to tackle any challenge that comes their way.

PRACTICE COURAGEOUS CONVERSATIONS

Have those difficult conversations you've been avoiding. Whether it's giving constructive feedback, addressing a conflict, or standing up for what you believe in, approach these conversations with courage and compassion. Remember, courageous conversations can lead to meaningful change and strengthen relationships.

SEEK OUT DISCOMFORT

Step out of your comfort zone and embrace new challenges. Volunteer for projects that stretch your abilities, try new ways of doing things, and welcome the opportunity to learn and grow. Remember, growth and innovation happen outside of your comfort zone. By seeking out discomfort, you'll become more adaptable, more resilient, and more confident in your ability to handle whatever comes your way.

FIND YOUR CREW

Surround yourself with a supportive network of mentors, peers, and friends who cheer you on and challenge you to be your best self. Lean on them for guidance, encouragement, and a listening ear when you need it most. Remember, you don't have to go it alone – having a crew sailed with you as you conquer the 7Cs of leadership is so much better. Your crew is there to support you, inspire you, and help you navigate the challenges of leadership.

CELEBRATE YOUR COURAGEOUS ACTS

Acknowledge and celebrate your courage, no matter how small the act. Keep a courage journal and write down your courageous moments each day. Reflect on how they made you feel and the impact they had on others. Celebrating your courage not only boosts your confidence but also inspires others to be courageous in their own lives.

CASE STUDY

THE COURAGE TO CONFRONT

Act I: The Early Days of Leadership

Picture this: it's my first year as a leader, and I'm just 24 years old. I'm full of enthusiasm but facing an uncomfortable challenge. One of my team members had a body odor issue and the entire team was complaining. The question was, as a leader, what would I do? The answer seemed obvious: talk to the person. But I had no idea how to approach such a delicate subject.

This was the worst conversation I had to face as a young leader. I felt terrible about it, but my mentor, Alyson, gave me invaluable advice: "As a woman, wouldn't you want to know?" Her words resonated with me, but I still did not know how to approach a team member without shaming her and embarrassing myself.

Act II: The Courageous Conversation

With Alyson's support, I mustered the courage to have the difficult conversation. I approached it with empathy, understanding, and honesty. The first conversation was tough, but it was necessary. This was the beginning of my journey into courageous leadership. Alyson encouraged me to face such challenges directly, emphasizing the importance of honesty and openness.

As the years passed, I became adept at handling sensitive issues. I was often the designated deliverer of difficult news in our town halls, a role I embraced as a leader. Each conversation, no matter how uncomfortable, helped me grow stronger and more confident.

Act III: Coaching Courage Today

Fast forward to today, and I apply the same principles when coaching my leadership and business clients. Whether they're running a business or managing a team within an organization, I teach them the importance of courage in leadership.

My coaching strategy is straightforward: be honest, open, and factual. Remove the emotions and focus on what I call the SBI Technique—Situation, Behaviour, Impact. This method allows leaders to address the issue at hand without making it personal. It's about understanding what is happening, the impact it has, and the behavior that needs to change.

The Power of Courageous Leadership

One of my clients—let's call her Sara—faced a similar situation. She had to address a performance issue with a long-time employee. Using the SIB technique, Sarah was able to have an honest and impactful conversation that led to positive changes in her team.

In another instance, a business owner named James needed to communicate a significant change to his staff. He was anxious about the potential backlash but applied the principles of courageous leadership. By being transparent and focusing on the situation and its impact, he was able to guide his team through the transition smoothly.

These stories underscore the importance of courage in leadership. Courageous leaders face difficult situations head-on, with honesty and empathy. As leaders, it's our responsibility to have these conversations, no matter how uncomfortable they may be.

In conclusion, courageous leadership is a journey. It starts with a single difficult conversation and grows with each challenge faced and overcome. By embracing honesty, focusing on the situation, impact, and behavior, and removing emotions, we can navigate even the toughest situations with grace and strength.

COACHING MOMENT

Courage is like a muscle – the more you use it, the stronger it gets. Keep challenging yourself, seeking out new opportunities to be courageous, and inspiring others to do the same. Before you know it, courage will become second nature to you, and you'll be leading with confidence and conviction every day. What do you need to do to make strides in this difficult area of leadership?

SONG CHOICE

"Brave" by Sara Bareilles

This uplifting song encourages listeners to be brave and true to themselves, highlighting the importance of courage in facing life's challenges.

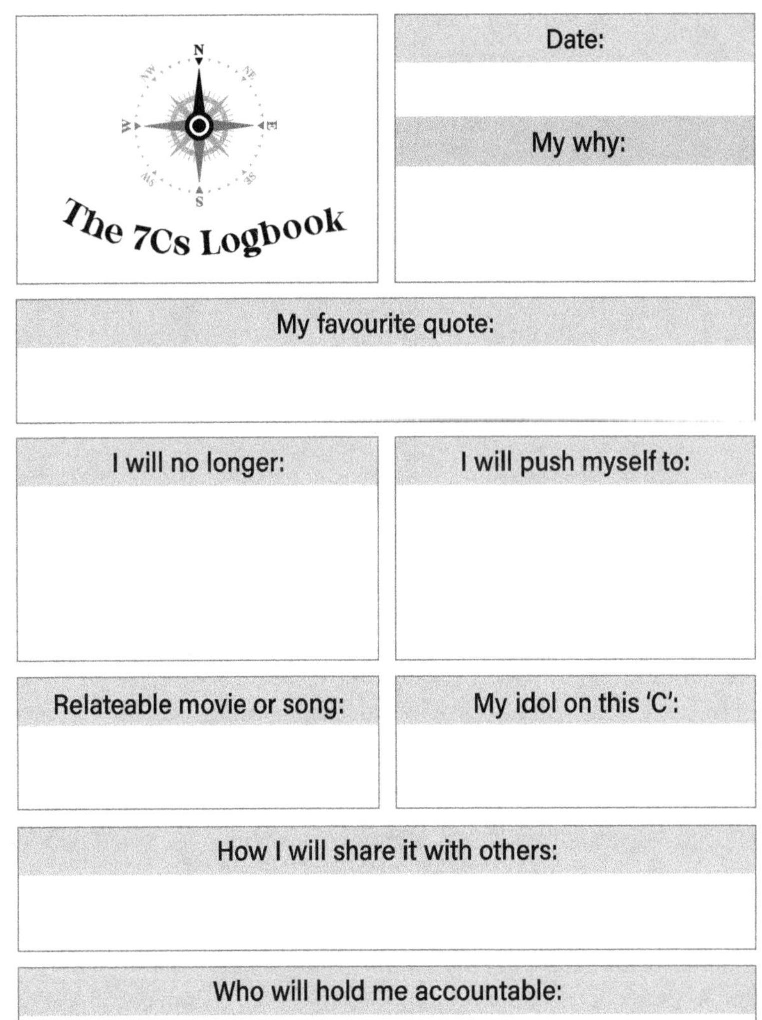
N
NW
NE
W
E
SW
SE
S
The 7Cs Logbook
Date:
My why:
My favourite quote:
I will no longer:
I will push myself to:
Relateable movie or song:
My idol on this 'C':
How I will share it with others:
Who will hold me accountable:

7c
CUSTOMER EXPERIENCE

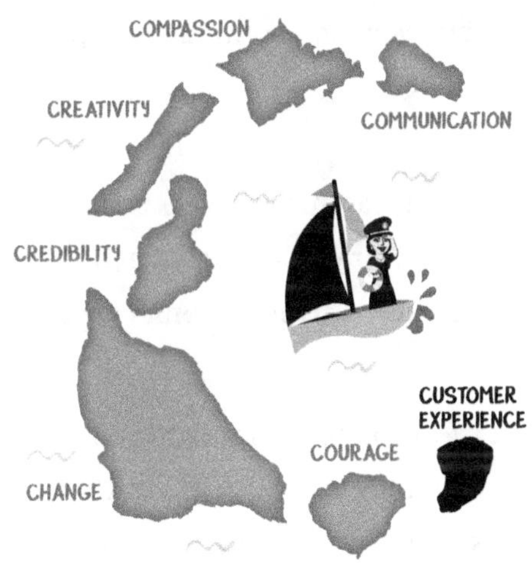

"Get closer than ever to your customers, so close in fact that you tell them what they need well before they realize it themselves."

- Steve Jobs

CUSTOMER EXPERIENCE CODE

- Understand the power of the customer experience and create a customer centric culture
- Harness technology
- Measure success and continually improve

Ah—one of my favourite topics is the customer experience. Now, I hear you asking: what on earth does leadership have to do with the customer experience? Well stay tuned!

If you take care of your customers, they in turn will take care of your good name. Going into business in 2014, one of the most important pieces for me was to create an exceptional, never-done-before-in-my-industry customer experience. And did I succeed? Just ask my clients!

Wherever you are in the world reading this book, have you noticed that the customer experience with many businesses have slipped? Here in Canada, Toronto especially, it has been a slow decline. Sloppy, substandard service is far from the exception. Many in customer service seem to work only for tips. In our very famous Canadian coffee shops, those that are part of a very popular franchise, you practically have to beg them for a sleeve for your coffee and if you're lucky, you may get ketchup for your sandwich. It's like you are asking for their first-born child! Yes, I know what you are thinking: "Coach, you said to have compassion!"—and I do. We all have bad days, however, when you choose to be in the service industry you need to leave your problems at the door.

At an insurance conference where I was honoured to be invited to speak, one of the agency leaders said, "Snow White never has a bad day." Imagine going to Disney and Snow White is sad and miserable. Unimaginable. Same goes for your own customer experience. Make sure you and your team are like Snow White.

I work hard with my clients to ensure they are all exceptional at the customer experience. This is one place where I've found they have all raise the bar far higher than I have set it for them. And guess what? They all have return clients and great reviews. Ensuring you focus on the customers is a sure way to ensure that the sales flood gates are open!

I attended Robin Sharma's in person events over many years and the service from his team and the event was by far the best I have ever experienced. I strive to be that good. Books on our table after each break. Massages. Encouragement to stretch—another way of looking out for our comfort and the best food all hosted at one of the best hotels: the Ritz Carlton. At the Ritz Carlton, they even de-seeded our lemons!

Now that is service.

Service = Leadership = Servant leadership. If you serve you will sell, hands down, providing your service and reasons you provide a high level of service are authentic.

Now, how about if you are leading a team? Perhaps you have external and internal customers. Your reputation as a leader starts internally amongst your peers. Do you want to be seen as someone who can be trusted to get things done? Or do you keep folks waiting for answers. Being trusted to do the right things at the right time: that's leadership.

Back in the day (when I worked in a bank), I was the queen of handling complaints from clients. I was a patient listener. And would leave no stone unturned to serve my team and customers. Once a client was yelling at me for a full five minutes, and I was silent. Then he said, "are you still there?"

"Yes, Sir," I replied. "I was just listening to you"

Everyone deserves to be heard, clients internal and external.

In a different chapter, I mentioned the movie, Castaway, starring Tom Hanks who plays a FedEx employee who gets stranded on a deserted island and uses his wits, resilience, and creativity to save himself. I love the part in the movie when once back in civilization, he returns a FedEx parcel to its rightful owner after all those months where he was at risk of dying on the island.

Now that's service!

How can we go the extra mile for our clients? What are some things you do already that work well, and where is there room for improvement? The trick is to ask a lot of questions and then to do this—I like to call this the Platinum Rule: you treat clients how they want to be treated.

I once took a flight back to Canada on a low budget airline that happened to share similar branding to my own company: everything was pink. The reputation and reviews were awful, but it only took one flight attendant who fully stepped into her leadership role (without a grand title I might add) to make it an exceptional experience for me. She, like the posh hotel in Toronto, de-seeded my lemon wedges and went the extra mile with a smile. I saw her at the back of the aircraft scrubbing a child's vomit from the floor and guess what—she was still smiling, putting the child's parents at ease, and taking pride in her work.

As I write this chapter I am seated in business class of our nation's famous airline. Now today I am lucky to have an amazing flight attendant who clearly loves her job. The lounge on the other hand left a lot to be desired. The staff there had little or no interest in their clients and while I was there, I did not see any of the staff even crack a smile. Therefore, from a customer experience and brand viewpoint, there isn't consistency. If you are in the people business, it needs to be all about the customer period.

Here are a few of my favourite coaching tips on this topic;

MAP OUT THE ADVENTURE:
UNDERSTANDING YOUR CUSTOMER'S JOURNEY

Just like planning a thrilling expedition, leaders need to map out every step of their customer's journey. From the first discovery to the final purchase and beyond, understanding these stages is crucial.

HEARTFELT CONNECTIONS:
THE POWER OF EMPATHY IN CUSTOMER RELATIONSHIPS

Picture this: You step into your customer's shoes and see the world through their eyes. That's empathy! It's the secret sauce to creating lasting connections and meeting their needs.

CULTURE IS KING:
CREATING A CUSTOMER-CENTRIC KINGDOM

Building a customer-centric culture is like constructing a majestic castle. It starts with a strong foundation of values and grows with every interaction, making your kingdom a beacon of customer delight."

STANDARDS OF EXCELLENCE:
SETTING THE BAR FOR CUSTOMER SERVICE

As leaders, we are the architects of exceptional service. Set the bar high, empower your team, and watch as they exceed even your wildest expectations.

FEEDBACK FEASTS:
NOURISHING GROWTH THROUGH CUSTOMER INPUT

Feast on feedback! It's the fuel that drives innovation and improvement. Listen to your customers, adapt to their needs, and watch your business flourish. Ask them for feedback, good bad or indifferent, this helps you to improve.

LEAD WITH GUSTO:
INSPIRING A CUSTOMER-FIRST CULTURE

Lead by example, not by decree! Show your team what it means to put the customer first, and they'll follow suit, creating a ripple effect of exceptional service.

MEASURE WHAT MATTERS:
USING METRICS TO DRIVE CUSTOMER SUCCESS

Numbers tell a story, and in the world of customer experience, they're your compass. Measure customer satisfaction, loyalty, Elevating the Customer Experience as a Leader

As a leader, your influence extends beyond your team; it reaches your customers, shaping their perception and experience with your brand. In this chapter, we'll delve into the importance of the customer experience, and how you, as a leader, can elevate it to new heights.

The Power of the Customer Experience

Think of your customer experience as a journey—a journey that begins the moment a customer interacts with your brand and continues long after. Every touchpoint, from the first impression to post-purchase support, shapes their perception of your brand and influences their loyalty.

As a leader, you are the driving force behind your team's customer-centric mindset. Your actions and behaviors set the tone for how your team interacts with customers. By demonstrating empathy, understanding, and a commitment to excellence, you inspire your team to do the same.

Elevating the customer experience requires more than just individual efforts; it requires a cultural shift within your organization. Encourage your team to prioritize the customer in everything they do, from product development to customer service.

Harness technology as it plays a crucial role in enhancing the customer experience. From CRM systems that track customer interactions to AI-powered chatbots that provide instant support, technology can streamline processes and personalize experiences.

Measure Success and Continuously Improve

To ensure your efforts are paying off, it's essential to measure the impact of your customer experience initiatives. Use metrics like Net Promoter Score (NPS), customer satisfaction (CSAT), and customer lifetime value. As a business owner, Google reviews and testimonials are at the heart of my business and take the honest temperature of those who I have served.

The customer experience is not static; it's ever evolving. Encourage your team to continuously seek feedback, analyze data, and iterate on their strategies to ensure they are meeting the evolving needs and expectations of your customers. As a leader, you have the power to transform the customer experience and create lasting impressions that drive loyalty and advocacy. By prioritizing the customer, leading by example, and fostering a customer-centric culture, you can elevate your brand above the competition and create meaningful connections that last a lifetime, and retention to ensure your journey leads to success.

 *Whatever you do, do it well. Do it so well that when people see you do it, they will want to come back and see you do it again, and they will want to bring others and show them how well you do what you do." - Walt Disney*

Disney Class Customer Service

I would be missing a huge customer experience moment if I didn't talk about Disney, its incredible theme parks, and their world-renowned, exceptional customer service. I would highly encourage you to add this to your bucket list if you haven't yet taken a trip there. You might think it's just for children, but alas, the big mistake we make as adults is forgetting to play in our lives! During numerous Robin Sharma live events we would design our vision boards using crayons, to get the creativity flowing. Sometimes you just need to think like a child and be carefree. Going to Disney just might be what you need to give you the ultimate standard in customer care. Perhaps you can even write a trip off as a tax expense!

It is truly a place where dreams do come true. The moment you walk through the gates, it's showtime for their cast. Remember the analogy "Snow White never has a bad day"? Imagine if she did. During one trip my daughter was small and was a Disney addict (a secret she still is to this day and a huge Donald Duck fan). It was our first time staying in the Disney resorts—and wow. All the garbage cans were white and pristine with not a speck of dirt or mess on them. Such impressive attention to detail

Disney's magic lies in the details. You will not fail to notice how clean the parks are or how perfectly themed each area is. The cast can't do enough to make your stay just perfect. I was more than happy to pay for exceptional service, here take my money! Side note regarding sales: consumers will pay more for an exceptional customer experience—but that's another book altogether. However, do consider this in your day-to-day experience with clients. Service sells.

One of my big audacious goals and dreams is to attend training at the Disney Training Institute in order to learn how to deliver the best from the best. One day I will do this so I can pass all the knowledge back to my clients. However, based on my research and years of park experiences, here is my take on their secret sauce:

TRAINING AND EMPOWERMENT

Disney's Cast Members are the heart and soul of the experience. They undergo extensive training to anticipate and exceed guest expectations. Whether it's a janitor or a ride operator, every Cast Member is empowered to create magical moments. I remember one instance where a Cast Member, seeing a child drop their ice cream, quickly appeared with a new one, free of charge. It's these small acts that leave a lasting impression.

CRAFTING THE MAGIC: STORYTELLING AND IMMERSION

At Disney, you don't just visit attractions, you step into stories. Each ride, show, and even the park layout is designed to immerse you in different worlds. When you're on Pirates of the Caribbean, you're not just on a ride—you're in a pirate's adventure. This level of immersion makes guests active participants in the magic.

EMOTIONAL CONNECTION

Disney excels at creating emotional connections. Think about the joy of meeting Mickey Mouse or the nostalgia of riding "It's a Small World." These experiences are designed to tug at your heart-strings and create memories that last a lifetime. I'll never forget the look on my child's face when they met their favorite princess. It was pure joy.

LEADERSHIP LESSONS FROM DISNEY: CUSTOMER-CENTRIC CULTURE

Disney's leadership is all about putting the guest first. Every decision is made with the guest experience in mind. They are constantly innovating based on feedback to ensure each visit is better than the last. This guest-first approach is a powerful lesson for any leader.

LEADING BY EXAMPLE

Disney leaders are often seen in the parks, engaging with guests and Cast Members alike. They listen, observe, and lead by example. This hands-on approach shows their commitment to the guest experience and sets a standard for everyone in the organization.

THE IMPACT OF EXCEPTIONAL EXPERIENCE: GUEST LOYALTY

Disney's dedication to customer experience fosters incredible loyalty. Guests return year after year, bringing new generations with them. Loyal guests become ambassadors, sharing their magical experiences with others.

BUSINESS SUCCESS

All this magic translates into significant business success. Happy guests spend more, return more often, and spread the word. Disney's exceptional customer experience drives ticket sales, merchandise purchases, and a robust brand reputation.

BRINGING DISNEY MAGIC TO YOUR LEADERSHIP: CONSISTENCY AND STANDARDS

One key lesson from Disney is the importance of consistency. Maintain high standards in every interaction and detail. It's this unwavering commitment to quality that ensures guests always leave happy.

INNOVATION AND ADAPTABILITY

Never stop innovating. Disney continually updates its attractions and experiences to keep them fresh and exciting. Visiting Disney World is more than just a fun trip: it's a masterclass in customer experience and leadership. By embracing their philosophy of attention to detail, storytelling, and guest-centric culture, we can all create magical experiences in our fields. So, the next time you're leading a team or serving a customer, think about how you can sprinkle a little Disney magic into everything you do. Adapt, and always strive to improve.

Let me go and get my wand!

CASE STUDY

CUSTOMER EXPERIENCE -
Transforming Complaints into Opportunities

In the fast-paced world of banking, I was strategically seated just outside the office of one of our most senior leaders. The reason? I was known as the Queen of Complaints. Any grievance that reached their desk inevitably ended up on mine because I had a knack for turning complaints into opportunities. How did I achieve this? Through exceptional listening skills and the ability to view complaints not as problems, but as magic moments to create wins for the company.

Act I: The Queen of Complaints

Picture this: a bustling bank office, phones ringing, and a constant stream of clients. During this, my desk was a hub of activity. This simple example bears repeating—one day, a client called, his voice booming with anger. He was furious about an issue with his account and started yelling at the top of his lungs. I remained silent, letting him vent. When he finally paused, there was a moment of stunned silence. "Uh, hello? Are you still there?" he asked.

"Yes, Sir, I'm here. I was just listening to you," I replied calmly.

This mindful act of listening had a profound effect. It diffused his anger and allowed me to address his concerns effectively. By validating his feelings and providing a solution, I turned a potentially disastrous situation into a positive experience.

Act II: The Art of the Customer Experience

Fast forward to my entrepreneurial journey, and the customer experience remains the cornerstone of my business philosophy. One client stands out. Let's call her "Jane". Jane has been with me since the inception of her business. Her success can be traced back to one key principle: an unwavering focus on the customer experience.

Jane's approach is refreshingly simple. There are no complex sales funnels or fancy marketing tactics. Instead, she puts herself out in front of her community, being authentic, real, and genuinely serving her customers. Her strategy? Listening to her clients, understanding their needs, and delivering exceptional service.

Act III: The Power of Authenticity

One day, Jane faced a challenging situation with a disgruntled customer. The customer was upset about a delayed delivery. Jane, drawing from the principles she learned, listened patiently to their concerns. After acknowledging the issue, she went above and beyond to rectify the situation, even offering a personalized apology and a small token of appreciation. This act of kindness not only resolved the issue but also turned the client into a loyal advocate for Jane's business.

Epilogue: Servant Leadership

Through my experiences at the bank and in my own business, I've learned that the customer experience is paramount. It's about more than just resolving complaints; it's about creating memorable interactions that build trust and loyalty. Jane's story is a testament to this. By being a servant to others, she has carved out her space in the leadership pool of her field.

In conclusion, the art of listening and genuine service can transform any situation into a win. As leaders, it's our responsibility to champion the customer experience, ensuring that every interaction leaves a lasting positive impression.

COACHING MOMENT

So, what was your biggest takeaway? What do you need to do to improve yourself in this area or your teams? What can you implement immediately for success and to delight your customers?

As a leader, you have the power to transform the customer experience and create lasting impressions that drive loyalty and advocacy. By prioritizing the customer, leading by example, and fostering a customer-centric culture, you can elevate your brand above the competition and create meaningful connections that last a lifetime.

SONG CHOICE

"Happy" by Pharrell Williams

This song exudes positivity and happiness, reflecting the importance of customer satisfaction and the joy that comes from serving others.

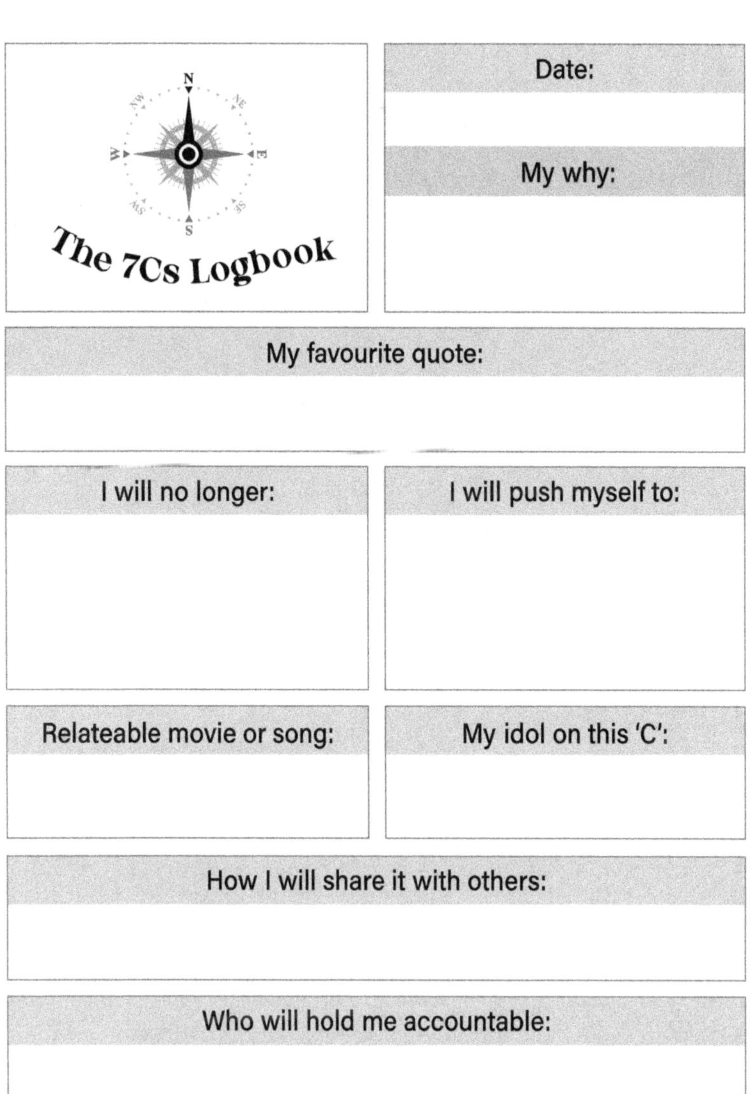

The 7Cs Logbook

Date:

My why:

My favourite quote:

I will no longer:

I will push myself to:

Relateable movie or song:

My idol on this 'C':

How I will share it with others:

Who will hold me accountable:

ACKNOWLEDGMENTS

I am deeply grateful to my amazing beta readers – Judi, Alyson, Chris, and DB. Your insightful and honest feedback has been invaluable in shaping this book. Your guidance and dedication have truly elevated this work, and I cannot thank you enough for your time and wisdom.

Thanks to Heather and Lana at Big World Creative for designing the stunning cover and graphics. You took my ideas and turned them into something beautiful, and I'm so grateful for your talent and vision. To Egor, your expertise with the website and landing page has been invaluable – thank you for bringing it all together so seamlessly. Tammy for your marketing and social media creativity.

To Akosua of What's Your Story-Author Services, my incredible editor, and support throughout this journey, your insights and patience have been instrumental, and I am thrilled with the final product.

Monica, my first leader and dance teacher, your influence continues to inspire me. I carry the lessons I learned from you into my work every day. Diane, your dance teaching and allowing me to teach your students was an invaluable lesson.

My clients who support everything I do, I love you all!

To everyone I've had the privilege of working with over the last 25 years in business and leadership – thank you for contributing to my growth and shaping me into the leader I am today.

And finally: thank you to my dear husband and daughter who graciously and lovingly allowed me the space to write this and brought me inspiration and cups of tea when they sensed I needed it.

ABOUT THE AUTHOR

Claudine Pereira was born in the UK, where her passion for dance and leadership began at Mo's Place in Reading. After moving to Canada in 1995, she embarked on a successful corporate leadership career. During this time, Claudine also excelled in Ballroom and American Rhythm dance, winning numerous competitions and frequently taking the top spot on the podium.

In 2014, Claudine founded The Pink Coach, a business and leadership coaching company serving clients in Canada and the UK. She is dedicated to helping leaders unlock their potential and achieve success. Claudine currently resides in Toronto with her husband, her daughter, and their beloved cat, Smokey. 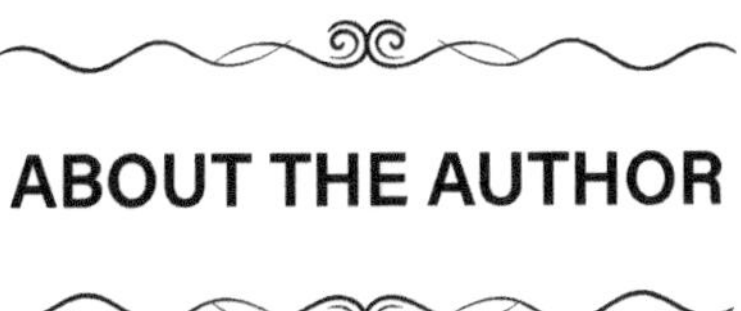

Claudine is a co-author of the 2017 bestselling book, *Live Out Loud (The Sisterhood Folios Book 1)*. This is her second book.

www.ingramcontent.com/pod-product-compliance
Lightning Source LLC
Chambersburg PA
CBHW060937050726
47592CB00003B/998